Nazi Foreign Policy, 1933–39

Seán Lang

Advanced
Topic*Master*

Series editors
Nicolas Kinloch
Seán Lang

Acknowledgements

My thanks got to Theo Schulte and Nicolas Kinloch for their advice on the content and structure of this book.

Philip Allan Updates, an imprint of Hodder Education, an Hachette UK company, Market Place, Deddington, Oxfordshire OX15 0SE

Orders

Bookpoint Ltd, 130 Milton Park, Abingdon, Oxfordshire OX14 4SB
tel: 01235 827720
fax: 01235 400454
e-mail: uk.orders@bookpoint.co.uk
Lines are open 9.00 a.m.–5.00 p.m., Monday to Saturday, with a 24-hour message answering service. You can also order through the Philip Allan Updates website: www.philipallan.co.uk

ISBN 978-1-84489-639-4

Impression number   5   4   3   2   1

Year   2013   2012   2011   2010   2009

The cover photograph, which shows Hitler entering the Sudetenland in 1938, is reproduced by permission of London Illustrated News.

Printed in Spain

Hachette UK's policy is to use papers that are natural, renewable and recyclable products and made from wood grown in sustainable forests. The logging and manufacturing processes are expected to conform to the environmental regulations of the country of origin.

P01462

Contents

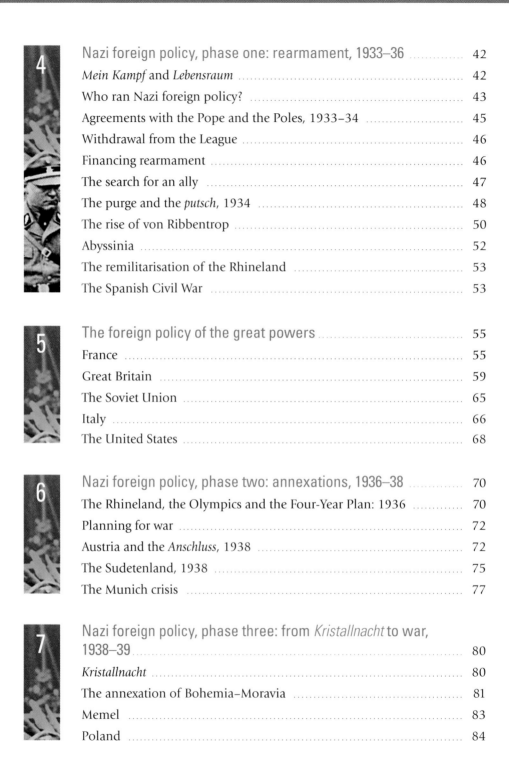

Introduction: seeing the wider picture

Easily the most common and most serious mistake a student can make in looking at Nazi foreign policy is to focus on it too narrowly. Especially if they have studied the period at GCSE, most students will have in mind a rough outline of such events of the 1930s as the reoccupation of the Rhineland in 1936, the *Anschluss* 2 years later, the Sudetenland crisis in 1938, and the dispute over the Polish Corridor that led to war in September 1939. These, however, are only some of the events of the period. Any account of the crisis of security in 1930s Europe should also include the 1934 uprising in Austria, the Italian invasion of Abyssinia and the Spanish Civil War, not to mention internal events within major states, such as the purges in Russia and the German Four-Year Plan. The economic situation needs to be given its due significance, too. Students who happily cite the impact of the Wall Street Crash as one of the factors that helped Hitler come to power in January 1933 often blithely talk about the political events of the rest of the decade without so much as a mention of the worldwide economic depression.

Other problems facing students are reflected in the title of this book, *Nazi Foreign Policy. Was* there in fact a single Nazi foreign policy on which all parties within the German government agreed? Was any such policy really Hitler's? And did Hitler have a set plan for foreign policy in the first place? None of these questions can be answered quite as simply as students often assume. Readers also need to be aware that, if they are to understand how it was that world war broke out in September 1939, they cannot study Nazi foreign policy in isolation from the German foreign policy of the 1920s, which was of obvious relevance to policy in the following decade, especially as, for most of the time, the same people within the German foreign ministry were running it. It is also taking too narrow a geographical perspective to concentrate on the policy of Germany alone, or just Germany and Britain, reducing other countries to caricatures with no real influence on events.

It does not take much thought to see why such a narrow focus is so inadequate. For example, it is often pointed out that in 1936, when he sent troops to reoccupy the Rhineland, Hitler told his troop commanders to withdraw immediately if there was any sign of military movement by the

French. In other words, French policy and intentions were crucial to him, as they should be to students writing about the period today. Similarly, students writing essays about Chamberlain's policy of appeasement tend to show they know that Britain's military resources were limited, yet seldom spot the obvious corollary to this: that Britain was therefore inevitably relying heavily on French military strength. It is obviously important to have at least a brief look at the position of France in the 1930s. Why did France, the senior military partner in the western alliance, apparently sit back and let Chamberlain do all the talking in 1938? Why didn't we hear more from the French during the crises of the 1930s? Like the famous dog that did not bark in the night, it is France's silence just when it should have been making a lot of noise that ought to attract our interest.

Similarly, the United States and the Soviet Union, two powers of global significance by anyone's reckoning, hardly feature in most students' analyses of the 1930s. In the case of America, the objection is usually made that the United States was too occupied with pulling itself through the Depression to pay much attention to Europe and its problems, and was too isolationist in any case. There is some truth in the first of these points, but the second cannot be taken at face value. The United States did have a foreign policy, and it certainly did not involve allowing Germany to dominate the continent of Europe. In the 1920s, close ties with the United States had been central to Gustav Stresemann's foreign-policy aims. It was clear to the Germans even before 1939 that American neutrality would be of a pro-British variety, as indeed it proved. Even though the United States was not going to intervene militarily in the crises of the 1930s, Hitler could not afford to ignore or forget the Americans and he knew it.

As for the Russians, to whom both sides turned rather belatedly in summer 1939, the fact that they did not participate directly in some of the big set-piece events of the 1930s does not mean that students can afford to ignore them. Some people at the time saw the decision not to invite Stalin to the Munich conference in 1938 as a major gaffe, a reflection of Chamberlain's deep suspicion of Soviet communism. Since Hitler had made it clear in *Mein Kampf* (insofar as anything in *Mein Kampf* can be described as clear) that *Lebensraum* was to be found in Russia, students should certainly give some thought to Stalin's outlook on the familiar events of the 1930s.

The questions of whether or not there was a single Nazi foreign policy, how it related to German foreign policy before 1939, and what was driving the other powers in the 1930s, will all be dealt with in this book — as will three common misconceptions about this period of history. I have termed the first of these the 'Munich myth', although it applies to the whole period. This is the popular conception of the events of the 1930s, centred on the idea that Chamberlain's policy of appeasement, as practised at Munich in 1938, was a disastrous and

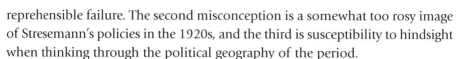

reprehensible failure. The second misconception is a somewhat too rosy image of Stresemann's policies in the 1920s, and the third is susceptibility to hindsight when thinking through the political geography of the period.

For easy reference, terms and names defined in the Glossary are highlighted in purple the first time they appear in each chapter.

Seán Lang

The 'Munich myth'

In 2003, when Tony Blair and George W. Bush were planning their invasion of Iraq, they justified their position by comparing the Iraqi president, Saddam Hussein, to Hitler and declaring that they drew inspiration from the example of Winston Churchill's stand against the policy of appeasing the German dictator in the 1930s. Twenty years earlier, when the military government of Argentina launched an invasion of the British Falkland Islands, Britain's prime minister Margaret Thatcher angrily snapped to the US Secretary of State Alexander Haig, who had proposed that the British negotiate with the Argentinians, that the desk she was sitting at was the one from which Neville Chamberlain had betrayed a small country to a bullying dictator and that she had no intention of following his example. 'We do not appease dictators,' she declared.

These examples neatly demonstrate the enormous difficulty facing students. The popular version of the events of the 1930s on which Thatcher, Blair and Bush were all drawing is deeply embedded in the consciousness of people around the world, and is to be met with in pubs, comedy shows, debating societies, radio and television news studios and all over the internet, as well as in government. Like all popular versions of history, it has the merit of being easy to follow, with strong, archetypal heroes, villains and victims. Its heroes are figures such as Churchill and Eden who stood out against the policy of appeasing Hitler. The villains are Hitler and his acolytes. The victims, apart from the millions of ordinary people around the world who would soon be caught up in the Second World War, are the small states of central Europe taken over by Germany in the 1930s: the Austrians (helped immeasurably by their 'good Germans' image in the Rodgers and Hammerstein musical *The Sound of Music*), the Czechs and the Poles. Centre stage are the appeasers themselves, led by Neville Chamberlain, the only man, jokers will tell you, who could hand over two medium-sized European states before breakfast.

The appeasers are not villains in quite the same way that Hitler and Mussolini are, but in their disastrously short-sighted policy they are the next worst thing. The most charitable people cast them as fools, out of their depth in deeper and more dangerous waters than they had imagined. The less charitably inclined see them as cowards, morally comparable to the dictators, to whom they airily handed over the defenceless peoples of central Europe. In 1940 a group of British left-wing writers produced a booklet attacking the appeasers, whom they wrongly considered a single homogeneous group, labelling them 'guilty men'; it took years before anyone seriously questioned the verdict.

This is a potent and well-established version of history and it takes more than the occasional student essay, however good, to overturn it. It received powerful reinforcement from Winston Churchill, himself a gifted amateur historian, who in retirement published a widely read account of the Second World War, which helped to establish his own, somewhat self-serving version of the events of the 1930s. Churchill called the volume dealing with the pre-war period *The Gathering Storm*, and in it he presented himself as a sort of prophet in the wilderness, warning repeatedly about the progress of German rearmament and the aggressive intentions of German foreign policy and meeting nothing but complacency, scorn or even active hostility from those in authority in Britain. Churchill's version suited the public mood in the 1950s and 1960s partly because it fitted the rather selective British public memory of exactly what had happened before the war, but also because it seemed to make perfect sense. The fact that appeasement had been unable to avert war and that Churchill had proved such a successful war leader seemed to his readers to justify his stance in the 1930s and to underscore the folly of those who had thought they could reach a deal with Hitler.

Central to this popular interpretation of events is a clear but simplistic under-standing of Hitler's foreign policy. It is widely assumed that Hitler was aiming at war all along and that the appeasers were foolish to try to do normal diplomatic business with him. In the years after 1945 it seemed to many on the victorious Allied side that the war was simply the latest episode in a tale of German aggression that stretched back through the twentieth century and into the century before. American troops occupying Germany were shown a propaganda film that talked of a series of three German Führers, starting with Bismarck's wars in the 1860s, going through the expansionist plans of Kaiser Wilhelm's government before 1914, and ending up with the Nazi period. British occupation forces were similarly told:

> But remember this: for the last hundred years — long before Hitler — German writers of great authority have been steadily teaching the necessity for war and glorifying it for its own sake. The Germans have much to learn.
> (2004) *Instructions for British Servicemen in Germany 1944*, Bodleian Library, p. 3.

In the 1950s it became common, following Churchill's usage, to speak of the 'first and second German wars', as if their causes could be explained entirely in German terms. However, as details of the horrors of the Nazi regime gradually emerged in the 1950s and 1960s, with the 1952 publication in English of *The Diary of Anne Frank* and the revelations about SS operations that came out of the trial of Adolf Eichmann in Jerusalem in 1961, the impression became firmly fixed in the public mind that there had been something uniquely evil about the Nazis that set them apart from earlier German regimes, however aggressive.

This interpretation was comforting for people in the former Allied countries as it reassured them that their wartime sacrifices had been in a good cause. It also helped to strengthen the sense of moral superiority common in western countries during the Cold War. The most widely read biography of Hitler in the 1950s and 1960s was Alan Bullock's significantly titled *Hitler: A Study in Tyranny*, published in 1952. Its central theme, the extraordinarily evil nature of Hitler and his regime, reinforced the general impression that the appeasers had been foolish, even wicked, not to take a stronger line with him.

The historical bombshells of 1961

This popular version of events remained the general consensus, including among liberal-minded Germans, until the publication in 1961 of two studies of twentieth-century Germany, which provoked storms of controversy, not only among historians. The German professor Fritz Fischer's influential study of the causes of the First World War, *Griff nach der Weltmacht: Die Kriegzielpolitik des kaiserlichen Deutschland 1914–1918* (published in English as *Germany's Aims in the First World War*, although *Germany's Drive for World Domination* would be a more accurate translation) argued that the Kaiser's Germany had planned aggressive war before 1914 and had aimed to dominate both Europe and the world. Although it provoked enormous controversy in Germany, where an attitude of 'at least we cannot be blamed for the First World War' prevailed, Fischer's thesis gained more ready acceptance in other countries. His condemnation of pre-1914 Prussian militarism fitted well with the anti-militaristic mood of young people in the Vietnam era.

Fischer's thesis also had profound implications for historians studying the origins of the Second World War. Its clear suggestion was that, although the Allies had drawn up the famous 'war-guilt clause' of the Treaty of Versailles to appease vengeful anti-German feelings among their populations and to serve as a legal cloak for reparations, they had, perhaps unwittingly, got it right: Germany *had* been to blame for causing the First World War. If this was true — and Fischer had impressive documentary evidence to support his accusation — then the central argument of those supporting appeasement (that the Treaty of Versailles had been too harsh on Germany) collapsed. Indeed, if Germany had deliberately provoked global war not once but twice, it suggested something deeply wrong in the German national psyche.

Unfortunately for those who like their heroes and villains easily differentiated, the Fischer thesis muddied the waters of the standard narrative of the 1930s. To start with, it called into question the general assumption that the Nazis had been uniquely evil. True, the Kaiser's Germany had not instituted mass murder on the scale of the Holocaust (although it did set about the virtual extermination of the Herero people of German South-West Africa), but if its warmongering was as blatant and self-serving as Fischer's evidence seemed to suggest, then Hitler fitted more neatly into a general pattern of German foreign policy than most historians and politicians had allowed for. This in turn suggested that the appeasers might have had more of a case than their critics recognised. After all, if Hitler was not so different from Bethmann-Hollweg, the German chancellor from 1909–17, then were Chamberlain and Halifax really to blame for dealing with him as they would with any other German statesman?

The second book to emerge onto the scene in 1961 dealt more directly with the 1930s. A. J. P. Taylor's *The Origins of the Second World War* stirred up a veritable hornets' nest of controversy and for years it dominated students' ways of looking at the period. To understand the book's impact, it is important to know something of Taylor himself. 'AJP', as he was popularly known, was an unorthodox historian, a specialist in the history of modern Europe and of Germany in particular, well known for his lively and provocative approach, which he deployed on television and in the popular press as well as in his historical works. A prominent member of the Campaign for Nuclear Disarmament, Taylor liked to see himself in the tradition of English radicals (the subject of his favourite among his own books, *The Troublemakers: Dissent Over British Foreign Policy 1792–1939*) and he enjoyed provoking his more stuffy academic colleagues, who did not think the tabloid press a proper place for a serious scholar to be writing. Taylor's writing style was based on well-turned phrases, often enshrining a paradox (the revolutionary year 1848, for example, was for him 'a turning point at which European history failed to turn') or confounding expectations in a manner reminiscent of the aphorisms of Oscar Wilde. The opening of his 1945 study, *The Course of German History*, became a celebrated, much parodied example of his style of exaggeration-to-provoke:

> The history of the Germans is a history of extremes. It contains everything except moderation, and in the course of a thousand years the Germans have experienced everything except normality…'German' has meant at one moment a being so sentimental, so trusting, so pious, as to be too good for this world; and at another a being so brutal, so unprincipled, so degraded, as to be not fit to live.
>
> Taylor, A. J. P. (1945) *The Course of German History*. Routledge, p. 1.

New slant on traditional views

It was this impish historian, with his taste for sweeping statements and for teasing provocation, who in 1961 produced the book for which he became best known, *The Origins of the Second World War*. Taylor refused to cast Hitler and the Nazis in their familiar role of evil superhumans and saw them as simply the latest in a long line of expansionist German nationalists. Arguably he saw them as less expansionist than earlier German leaders, because he presented Hitler's moves in the 1930s not as steps in a premeditated course towards war but as ad hoc reactions to events forced on him by others. Further turning traditional views on their head, Taylor presented Chamberlain as a skilful and pragmatic politician, with a much surer grasp on the realities of the situation than the intemperate and isolated Churchill. Taylor was dismissive of evidence that suggested Hitler was planning for war. He denied any clear link between *Mein Kampf*, which he dismissed as Hitler's daydreaming, and German foreign policy, and he was scathing about the famous Hossbach Memorandum, a report, written from memory after the event, of a top-level meeting in 1937 between Hitler and his military commanders in which Hitler apparently laid out in advance his plans for war with Germany's neighbours.

Much of the furore that surrounded the publication of *The Origins of the Second World War* came from Taylor's characteristic style of provocative over-statement. For example, it was widely accepted that Britain and France had been right to make a stand over Poland, yet Taylor held that it was unreasonable of them to do so when they had not taken a stand over Austria or Czechoslovakia. Moreover, he refused to cast the Czechs and Poles in their traditional roles as victims. To him, the Czech leader, Beneš, was a political schemer at the head of an artificial country and the Polish foreign minister, Beck, was an aggressive expansionist like Hitler, with his eyes on annexing the whole of Ukraine. Not only did Taylor suggest that Hitler's territorial demands were not necessarily as unreasonable as orthodox opinion held, but he came close to suggesting that Germany was in fact the aggrieved party when war broke out in 1939.

To some extent Taylor was being deliberately mischievous, playing with interpretations and terminology. More seriously, he completely discounted the importance of Nazi ideology in driving and directing Nazi foreign policy. To see why this matters, take the case of Poland. If you look at the long history of territorial shifts between Poland and Germany, the dispute over Danzig and the Polish Corridor becomes a straightforward irredentist struggle for former German territory: the Polish corridor constituted the heart of the old German state of Prussia. However, Hitler's contempt for the Poles was only partly dictated by traditional German nationalism. It was mainly fuelled by his racial beliefs, according to which the Poles were a sub-species of humanity whose destiny it was to serve the German 'master race'; racists do not make binding agreements with those they consider their racial inferiors. Not to take this into account is seriously to distort the way Hitler conducted his policy towards Poland.

Many of the pillars of Taylor's arguments have crumbled in the years since 1961. He has been criticised for his dismissive attitude towards the role the French played in events and for his underestimation of the role and significance of Mussolini. His denial that Hitler had any long-term plans for war, a view shared by few serious historians nowadays, was particularly upsetting for the generation that had come through the war, and occasioned an impassioned and emotional argument on television with the eminent historian of Nazi Germany, Hugh Trevor-Roper. Taylor's pithy paradoxes have been characterised as nice phrases that don't actually mean much, and his almost exclusive concentration on Britain and Germany is generally regarded as inadequate. Above all, his discounting of the importance of Nazi ideology, the crucial factor that set Hitler apart from earlier German expansionists, is generally seen as a fatal flaw in his argument. Nevertheless, his book is still required reading for students, mainly because it helps to shock them out of the easy assumptions of the popular version of history. Even if Hitler was planning war, it by no means necessarily follows that he was planning for the war he actually got: against Britain and France over the independence of Poland. Recognising the importance of Nazi ideology does not make the longer-term pattern of German foreign policy irrelevant. Moreover, some of Taylor's arguments have stood the test of time. Recent studies have been much more sympathetic to Chamberlain and have judged appeasement a pragmatic, some would even argue a successful, policy.

What, then, should students make of the Fischer and Taylor theses? The Fischer thesis certainly helps to place Hitler in the context of the political climate of his early years and of the diplomatic tradition within which the Nazis were working. It also guards against too easy an acceptance of the case against the Treaty of Versailles. The Taylor debate, although more directly relevant, is more problematic. At a general level, it is a clear demonstration that the period can be viewed differently from the popular version of events; it is also a reminder that even a single-minded leader such as Hitler cannot have everything his own way and is subject to the influence of other factors and other leaders. Ironically, perhaps, Taylor's *The Origins of the Second World War* is also a warning to the student not to commit the same sins of omission as he did, but to give proper consideration to factors other than policy-making and to look beyond the traditional focus on Britain and Germany, Chamberlain and Hitler.

If only Stresemann had lived…

Just as we like our narratives to be neat, with strong heroes and villains, so we also appreciate injecting a note of poignancy into them for extra pathos. In this case the poignant moment comes in 1929, the year of both the Wall Street Crash and the death from a heart attack of Gustav Stresemann, the statesman who pulled Germany out of the disastrous inflation of 1923. Stresemann has gained a reputation as the 'good German'. It was he who put the German economy back on an even footing, ushering in the economic boom of the 1920s, often known as the 'golden years' of the Weimar Republic, and re-established Germany's diplomatic relations with the other great powers, notably in the Locarno Treaties of 1925. It is often said that, if he had lived, Stresemann could have saved Germany from the effects of the Depression just as he saved it from inflation; if he had done that, the theory goes, the Germans would not have turned to Hitler, and if Hitler had not become chancellor of Germany the history of the twentieth century might have been different. (For an illustration of this way of regarding Stresemann's untimely death, see his entry at www.wikipedia.com.)

Well, maybe. Speculating about the what-might-have-beens of history is always agreeable and can be instructive. One such treatment has considered what might have happened had Stresemann lived beyond 1929: see Duncan Brack's *President Gore and Other Things That Never Happened* (2006, Politico). However, there are some serious objections to such 'counterfactual' thinking. To start with, it suggests we can trace a whole sequence of events following on from one specific factor. It is certainly reasonable to consider the difference Stresemann's survival would have made in the immediate term, but without hard evidence we cannot take our speculation forward more than a few weeks, a few months at most, beyond the date of his death. Quite apart from the possibility that we might have saved Stresemann from a heart attack only for him to walk under a Berlin tram, expecting everything to have been different because of a different fate for one man raises the question of how far events are dictated by individuals in the first place. Those who reject the 'great man' school of history in favour of the importance of wider social and economic forces would regard the death of an individual, even one as important as Stresemann, as a supreme irrelevance.

Even if we do accept the crucial importance of individuals in history, we cannot know how Stresemann would have responded to what happened to Germany in the period following his death; nor can we say with anything like certainty that he could have prevented the Nazis coming to power or the outbreak of the Second World War. To make such claims assumes that Stresemann would have had the answers for the Depression as he did for inflation, yet runaway inflation within an individual country is a very different business from a dramatic global trade collapse. Restoring confidence in money usually involves suspending the discredited currency until it can be replaced with a new one. Stresemann did this with the Reichsmark in 1923, calling it in and replacing it with the Rentenmark. Roosevelt applied the same idea to the American banking system 10 years later, closing all banks and allowing only federally backed ones to reopen. A similar policy was followed in the former East Germany, where, after German reunification in 1991, the worthless East German currency was called in and replaced with the western Deutschmark.

Solving the effects of the worldwide Depression was a different matter, and Stresemann might not have coped any better than his good friend and equally capable fellow economist, US President Herbert Hoover. As it was, Roosevelt's response to the crisis was the enormous public spending of the New Deal programme, to provide waged labour for America's unemployed and at the same time to build up the infrastructure of the American economy. If Stresemann was going to help Germany to recover, a similarly huge-scale programme of public works would have been the obvious policy for him to pursue. However, historians have long pointed out that Roosevelt's New Deal did not, in fact, solve the problem of the Depression, and where Roosevelt failed, with all the resources at his disposal, it would be rash to assume that Stresemann would necessarily have succeeded.

...could he have contained Hitler?

In any case, even a live and healthy Stresemann might not have been able to avoid a coalition with the Nazis in the fluctuating state of German politics in the late 1920s. Indeed, Hitler's government in 1933 was just such a coalition with the German Nationalists. We might think that Stresemann would have been at the head of such a coalition, but we cannot be certain and we cannot assume that he would somehow have been able to control or contain Hitler and his Nazi governmental colleagues any more than President Hindenburg or the other non-Nazis in Hitler's first cabinet were able to do. Perhaps Stresemann would have been eliminated in the Night of the Long Knives. Maybe he would have held his nose and stayed on, like Hitler's finance minister, Hjalmar Schacht, hoping to turn Hitler away from his most extreme policies by influence from inside. This is speculation, but the failure of everyone else, including Schacht, to exercise that sort of influence on Hitler does not encourage confidence that Stresemann would necessarily have succeeded.

Perhaps the most important corrective to the idea that Stresemann's survival would have changed the fate of the world is to look at his handling of foreign policy. At first sight, the contrast with Hitler could hardly be starker. Where Hitler was quite prepared to bully foreign dignitaries, Stresemann had a friendly, easy-going nature, which won him many friends, especially among the foreign statesmen with whom he had dealings. He was pragmatic enough to recognise that Germany would have to work within the terms of the Treaty of Versailles, and he negotiated two deals, the 1924 Dawes Plan and the 1929 Young Plan, to get Germany's reparations payments into a more manageable schedule. He negotiated the Locarno settlement with Britain and France, and in 1926 he got Germany accepted into the League of Nations. He was committed to peaceful diplomacy: in 1926 he shared the Nobel Peace Prize with the French prime minister, Aristide Briand, and in 1928 he signed up to the Kellogg–Briand Pact, by which signatories renounced the use of war to further their political ends.

All of this marked out his approach as different from the Nazis'. They rejected Versailles and denounced those who went along with it. When the Nazis talked about Stresemann's policy of 'fulfilment' of the treaty, it was not meant as a compliment. For that reason they also denounced the Dawes and Young Plans, even though they mitigated the effects of Versailles. They believed the proper response was to tear Versailles up. What the Nazis did not quite realise, perhaps, was the extent to which Stresemann had done just that. Getting Germany into the League was just as defiant of the terms of Versailles as was marching troops into the Rhineland. Stresemann undermined Versailles more than Hitler did because he persuaded the Allies, too, to move away from it. The supreme example of this was Locarno. Students often learn that at Locarno Stresemann accepted the western settlement but managed to get the east left open for revision. This is broadly true, but it misses the main point: simply getting the other powers to agree to meet at Locarno was effectively to tear up the Treaty of Versailles. A treaty is a binding agreement, the more so when it is dictated to a defeated power. A country cannot sign and then hope to come back later and renegotiate the parts it doesn't like. However, if all the parties to a treaty agree to reconvene to go over the issues, it is a sign that the original treaty is no longer considered sufficient.

In the case of Locarno, not only did the agreement leave the door open for the Germans to raise any issue relating to their eastern borders that they liked

— which is exactly what Hitler did in the 1930s — but it meant that both Britain and France had accepted that full application of the Treaty of Versailles was no longer practical. From then on it was France, not Germany, that was in the position of having signed a treaty and then regretting it, with the important difference that, whereas the Germans could legitimately complain that Versailles had been forced on them, the French could not say that of Locarno. Stresemann's style was completely different from Hitler's. He had no dreams of *Lebensraum* or master races, but the general tendency of Stresemann's foreign policy — to unshackle Germany from the Treaty of Versailles, restore its international prestige and regain its lands in the east — was very similar to Hitler's. Stresemann shared Hitler's low opinion of the Poles and even started a trade war with them in 1925 with a view to making Poland economically dependent on Germany and relieving it of former German lands. Anyone looking at what the Germans actually did to Poland in terms of its territory and economy after 1939 can see that, in their much more brutal manner, the Nazis were following much the same idea.

Questions

1 Why have historians found it so hard to arrive at an accurate interpretation of Nazi foreign policy?
2 How far do you agree with the claim of A. J. P. Taylor that the events of the period 1919–39 are 'a story without heroes; and perhaps even without villains'?
3 What was distinctively Nazi about German foreign policy in the period 1933–39?

The Great War and after

Nazi foreign policy and the other powers' reactions to it grew directly out of the experience of the First World War. It was not simply that the Nazis wanted to revise the settlement of the Treaty of Versailles — they were far from alone in wanting to do that — but also that the Nazis' larger vision in foreign policy and their views of other countries were rooted firmly in Germany's experience of war between 1914 and 1918.

War and policy

The Nazi government was unusual in that so many of its members had had frontline experience during the Great War. Hitler served as a private soldier, winning the Iron Cross and promotion to corporal; he always treasured the special bond that existed between men who had served together in the trenches. Other members of his government had also gone through the trenches, collecting wounds and Iron Crosses in fairly equal number. These men included von Papen (who was also active as a German spy), von Neurath, Roehm, von Ribbentrop and Goering, who had been a highly decorated combat pilot in the famous 'flying circus' of the Red Baron, Manfred von Richthofen. The Nazis also enjoyed the support of the celebrated German commander General Ludendorff and served in government under the presidency of Field Marshal von Hindenburg. If they did plan for European war, they were at least working from first-hand experience.

If the Great War had provided the Nazis with such extensive first-hand experience of war, why were they so keen to embark on another? This can be difficult to understand for people whose image of the Great War has been heavily influenced by the work of the British war poets and by film and television treatments such as *Oh! What a Lovely War* and *Blackadder Goes Fourth* (sic). In the immediate aftermath of the war this sort of bitter anti-militarist reaction did set in across Europe. Its most famous manifestation was the novel *All Quiet on the Western Front* by the German writer and war veteran Erich Maria Remarque, which was made into a successful film by Lewis Milestone in 1930.

Chapter 2

However, this attitude lasted much longer in the English-speaking world than on the continent, where attention quickly focused less on the experience of fighting the war than on the territorial settlement that resulted from it.

This difference in attitudes reflected two distinct conceptions about the nature of war itself: an 'Anglo-Saxon' one, current in Britain and the USA, and a continental one. The Anglo-Saxon view was that war was a regrettable necessity for which a nation should certainly be prepared but which it should not actively seek. The British view is encapsulated in a famous 1878 music-hall song whose chorus gave birth to the term 'jingoism', meaning an aggressive and pugnacious form of patriotism:

> We don't want to fight, but by jingo! if we do,
> We've got the ships, we've got the men, we've got the money too!

The significant words were not the threats at the end but the admission of unwillingness at the beginning. The Americans were deeply shaken by the slaughter of their Civil War (1861–65) and did not seek to engage in further large-scale fighting if they could avoid it. Woodrow Wilson won the 1916 presidential election on the ticket that he had kept America out of war.

The Balkan crisis, which gave rise to the 'by jingo!' song, ended in popular rejoicing not because the British had won a battle but because the Prime Minister, Benjamin Disraeli, went to a peace congress in Berlin and managed to extract a highly satisfactory settlement without the need to go to war at all. In a celebrated phrase Disraeli declared that he had brought home 'peace with honour'. Neville Chamberlain specifically referred to this example when he returned from the Munich conference in 1938, declaring that he, too, was bringing back from Germany peace with honour; he received much the same rapturous reception. For the British, the experience of the Great War, coming on top of the slaughter they had suffered in the Boer War (1899–1902) underlined their view that war should be waged only in the last resort after all other means of settling matters had been exhausted.

The continental conception of war, to be found in France, Italy and tsarist Russia and epitomised in Germany, compared it to an athlete's vigorous regime of healthy exercise. Whereas the British liked to stress the bloodless nature of major events in their history, these countries took pride in having forged themselves and their people through war. Bismarck said he had unified Germany through 'blood and iron'; the Italians gloried in the battles with Austria through which they had unified their country; and the French kept alive the memory of the days when Europe had trembled before Napoleon's armies. The Germans took to heart the maxim of the nineteenth-century general and theorist Carl von Clausewitz that war should not be regarded as an interruption of normal political operations, but as a legitimate means of advancing political ends. The ideal was decisive victory after a short, devastating campaign, a technique the Prussians perfected in a series of wars with their neighbours in the 1860s and 1870s. Other powers planned for similarly swift and decisive victory in the great European war they all confidently expected early in the new century.

When the Great War finally arrived, the Clausewitzean ideal proved impossible to achieve because techniques such as trench systems, barbed wire and heavy machine guns had given the advantage to the defender. However, technology also showed the way out of the impasse, with the development of tanks, bombing aircraft and submarines. Three inter-war writers, Charles de Gaulle in France, Basil Liddell Hart in Britain and Heinz Guderian in Germany, applied the Clausewitzean ideal to strategic thinking, combining air and land forces to paralyse the enemy. The Germans developed this idea into the strategy of *blitzkrieg* ('lightning war'). *Blitzkrieg* made the Clausewitzean ideal possible again and allowed states that thought in such terms, as Germany certainly did, to return to the idea of integrating short decisive wars into foreign policy thinking.

The German view of the British

The Germans had a strong sense of affinity with the British, with whom they had close links, both through the two countries' royal families (the Kaiser was half-English and proud of it) and through extensive German emigration to England during the nineteenth century. It was common for Germans in the 1900s to have spent time in England or to have relatives there, rather as it is nowadays for British people to have family links with Ireland, Australia or Pakistan. English literature, especially Shakespeare, was admired in Germany, the fine German translations of Shakespeare's work constituting a significant genre within German literature itself. Before 1914, German admiration for British power was mixed with anger that Britain seemed unwilling to step aside even a little to allow Germany its 'place in the sun', but during the war German soldiers viewed the British Tommies with considerable respect, even a certain amount of affection. Hitler himself served in the British sector of the western front, and once warmly welcomed a group of British war veterans to Berchtesgaden. Moreover, although any German soldier who faced the disastrous British attack on the Somme in 1916 would be conscious of the British capacity on occasion to bungle things badly, the Germans were also painfully aware that it was the British who had introduced the terrifying spectacle of tanks onto the battlefield, while the British naval blockade of German ports had reduced the country to virtual starvation. Popular opinion often attributed to the British an almost superhuman capacity for ingenious schemes to bring Germany down, and both the Weimar Republic and the Nazi regime sought to develop closer relations between the two countries. Even at the height of the Second World War it was common for British prisoners of war to report being told by their German captors that it was a tragedy that the two countries were at war and that Britain's natural place was at Germany's side against the Russians.

The German view of the French

The German attitude towards the French was more complex. Soldiers who fought at Verdun were in no doubt of the tenacity and courage of the French soldier, but the Germans also encountered the French as conquered civilians within the occupied area behind the front line, where incidents of resistance prompted savage reprisals. The Germans always had contempt for guerrilla or resistance activity, and it lowered their opinion of the French. In addition, the Germans were conscious that the Great War was the latest episode in a long tale of bitter rivalry between the French and Germans dating back more than 100 years. The famous eighteenth-century Prussian king Frederick the Great had made his name fighting the French. A generation later, Prussian military power was crushed by Napoleon, and the Germans never forgot that Napoleon's men had marched in triumph through Berlin. For the next half-century the Germans felt under threat from overwhelming French military power. One of the best-known German nationalist songs extolled the 'watch on the Rhine' against the French menace. By Bismarck's day it was widely believed that Germany could never establish itself as a genuine state until it had stood up to the French and humbled them, which is precisely what Bismarck did in the Franco-Prussian War of 1870–71. The Prussians, by planned use of the railway system, were able to invade France and defeat her forces in a matter of weeks. They then subjected Paris to an agonising 4-month siege and gathered all the kings and princes of Germany together in the Hall of Mirrors at Versailles, the symbol of French magnificence and power, to declare a unified German Reich; and imposed humiliating peace terms on France, which involved a heavy fine, a German army of occupation and the cession to Germany of the border provinces of Lorraine and Alsace. To add to the sweet taste of revenge, France had been led to this disastrous defeat by another Bonaparte, the emperor Napoleon III, who fled into ignominious exile in England.

In its opening months the Great War revived awful French memories of the 1870–71 conflict. Once again the Germans swept into France and headed for Paris, but this time the French were able to hold them on the Marne. It is no coincidence that the Marne became the subject of intense romanticised myth in France. Through all the long years of trench warfare the French never lost sight of the idea that the Great War would wipe out the memory of 1870–71. Everything about the peace settlement, not least the symbolism of signing the Treaty of Versailles in that same Hall of Mirrors, was designed to show the Germans that the old, powerful France was back. The Germans had better start watching on the Rhine again.

However, the Germans could take comfort from a dangerous weakness in their old enemy. Ever since the French Revolution (1789–99), France had been torn by deep and bitter internal divisions. After the defeat of 1871, Paris set up a radical socialist city authority called the Commune, and the French government sent troops in to crush it in scenes of appalling savagery and violence. The Germans witnessed the bloodbath, even helping the French government troops to find the best positions from which to bombard their own capital city. France's internal politics were no less bitter by 1914. The French socialist leader, Jean Jaurès, was assassinated on the very eve of war, and in 1917 the French army on the western front was hit by widespread mutiny. The Germans, whose own armed forces were crippled by mutiny in 1918, were in no position to feel smug, but the more patient or far-sighted among them knew that France's internal divisions might yet undermine the threat it undoubtedly posed to postwar Germany.

The German view of the Russians

The Germans, like the rest of Europe, regarded Russia as medieval and backward, a peasant country in an age of industrial might, but that did not make Russia any less dangerous, and the British certainly took Russian territorial expansion towards India seriously. Bismarck had sought to keep the Russian threat at bay by a three-way alliance of Germany, Russia and Austria–Hungary, but eventually had to abandon that idea and treat Russia as a potential enemy. The Germans' main fear was of a war in which they faced Russia in the east and France in the west, the famous 'war on two fronts', and the German general staff drew up complex schemes to avoid it. The most famous of these schemes was the Schlieffen Plan, devised by Alfred von Schlieffen, the German army's chief of staff, and designed to create two separate wars: a short, decisive one in the west against France, followed by a more drawn-out war in the east against Russia.

In the event, the war in the west proved more difficult, and the war in the east easier, than the planners had anticipated. Although the Russians did get their act together more quickly than von Schlieffen had allowed for, it still took them

3 weeks. The Germans were then able to outmanoeuvre, surround and almost annihilate two Russian armies at the battles of Tannenberg and the Masurian Lakes in 1914. Thereafter, although the war in the east dragged on as it did in the west, the Germans and Austrians seldom lost the advantage. The big Russian offensives, under Brusilov in 1916 and Kerensky the following year, either petered out or failed completely. It is perhaps no coincidence that von Hindenburg and Ludendorff, the German commanders in the east, quickly became national heroes.

The Bolshevik revolution seemed to do little to improve Russia's military position. The Germans were able to use their overwhelmingly superior position to put pressure on Trotsky to sign a humiliating peace treaty at Brest-Litovsk in 1918, giving Germany huge swathes of Russian territory. When war broke out between Russia and Poland the following year the Russians proved unable to defeat the Poles and had to sue for a compromise peace. The lesson many Germans drew about the Russians from the war was that, dangerous though Bolshevism might or might not be, and without underestimating the logistical problems of taking on such a vast and populous country, in military terms the Russians were not quite as formidable as they looked.

There was another school of thought about Russia. General von Seeckt, commander of the German army under the Weimar Republic, and Walther Rathenau, the foreign minister in 1922, saw Russia as a potential ally. They shared a romantic vision of a partnership between the great Germanic nation and the great Slavic nation, drawn both from history (Germans had played a major role in building modern Russia) and from the fact that, for different reasons, both states were pariah nations in the 1920s, excluded from the League of Nations and generally viewed with deep suspicion. The first concrete sign of this search for partnership came in 1922 with the Treaty of Rapallo. Von Seeckt, however, envisaged a much more active partnership in which the two states would crush the upstart state of Poland between them as they had done in the eighteenth century. To those who shared this vision, the political differences between Germany and the Soviet Union were of much less importance than the mutual benefit to be gained from cooperation. The Nazi–Soviet Pact of 1939, which should hardly have surprised anyone who had studied recent German politics, seemed to prove their point.

The German collapse in 1918

Students who look only at the battles of the Great War, especially from a British point of view, can find the German collapse in 1918 difficult to understand. The

British interpretation of the war was so heavily influenced by images of slaughter on the Somme or at Passchendaele that it is easy to get the impression that Britain was losing, and to assume that things must therefore have been going better for the Germans. This is not how it was. Britain's military effort was concentrated on the northern section of the western front. Germany, however, was losing men all along the western front and in the east. German losses, at 2,037,000 men (3.1% of the German population) dwarfed Britain's losses of 885,000 (1.9% of the population). More significantly, Germany's civilian population was suffering terribly from the effects of the British naval blockade. German civilian losses, at 426,000, were nearly four times the British figure. By autumn 1917 the German high command was well aware that Germany could not keep the war effort going for more than another year.

The moment when all likelihood of complete German victory disappeared came in April 1917 as the United States, not yet a great military power but with the resources to become one quickly, entered the war on the Allied side. From then on, the Germans' only realistic hope was to go all-out for as advantageous a position as possible so as to force the Allies into a compromise peace before American troops arrived in strength, which, it was calculated, was unlikely to happen before spring 1918. The Russian collapse in 1917 did not alter this situation as much as the Germans might have hoped because the provisional government's decision to keep Russia in the war prevented the Germans from transferring their eastern forces to the west for a whole year, a delay that effec-tively put paid to German hopes for a knockout blow in the west. The German western offensive in the spring of 1918 achieved total surprise and broke through the Allied lines, but the Germans did not have the resources or the will to follow the attack through. The Allies were thus presented with large numbers of German soldiers, tired, short of food and ammunition, cut off from their bases and without any prepared defensive positions. They then pushed them all the way back to the frontier, taking thousands of German prisoners, in one of the most successful military campaigns in history. When, on 29 September 1918, Ludendorff urged the Kaiser to abdicate, he added that he could not guarantee holding the military position even for 24 hours. Germany was facing a more complete collapse than at any time since Napoleon marched into Berlin.

The 'stab in the back'

Why, then, did the German people hold so strongly to the idea that Germany had not really been beaten, but had been 'stabbed in the back' by whichever scapegoats they wished to blame? Clearly an important part of the illusion came from the fact that the German high command had sued for peace before the Allies had actually crossed the German frontier. The German self-delusion was inadvertently fed by the Allies' decision not to seek a triumphant military parade through Berlin, which would only have continued the tit-for-tat pattern set by Napoleon and Bismarck. The idea of the virtuous hero who is treacherously stabbed in the back was deeply ingrained in German popular consciousness. In the traditional epic tale *The Ring of the Nibelung*, the subject of a fiercely nationalistic opera cycle by Richard Wagner, Siegfried, the Germanic hero, is stabbed in the back by an evil, half-human figure called Hagen of Tronje. The exact origin of the use of the term to describe Germany's collapse in 1918 is not clear. It seems to have been in circulation even before the war was over, but it was most often attributed to reports in the *Neue Zürcher Zeitung* in December 1918, and elsewhere in the German press the following year, of comments by the British General Maurice and a conversation between General Sir Neil Malcolm and Ludendorff.

Crediting the phrase to the British was important because it suggested it was not sour grapes on the part of the Germans but the sober judgement of an outside observer from an enemy country that the Germans respected. Malcolm seems to have done no more than summarise the situation that Ludendorff was describing to him, but that hardly mattered to those who would rather believe the theory than face up to the hard truth that Germany's proud military forces had met their match on the field of battle and lost.

Who exactly was supposed to have driven the dagger into Germany's unprotected back? The usual answers were 'politicians', 'socialists' and, increasingly, 'Jews'. Each is significant. The idea of a Jewish conspiracy had begun during the war, in 1916, when the German army commissioned a Jewish census, with which it tried (but failed) to show that Germany's Jews were not pulling their weight in the war. This idea of a conspiracy grew gradually through the 1920s, fuelled partly by Nazi propaganda but also by the fact that a number of leading Bolsheviks, including Trotsky, Zinoviev, Kamenev and Sverdlov, as well as Karl Marx himself, were of Jewish descent. The Nazis' coining of the term 'Jewish-Bolshevik' helped to fix in German minds the idea that Judaism and communism were somehow organically linked.

Blaming civilian politicians as a class was a reflection of the deep antipathy the German military felt for civilian politics. It also reflected the fact that US President Wilson had made the ending of the imperial government and the establishment of parliamentary democracy a condition of granting Germany a ceasefire. Thenceforth the military were able to claim that the Allies had unfairly imposed republican government on Germany. This detestation of civilian politics helps explain why the Nazis, without handing government over to the armed forces, made their regime look military, with military-style uniforms and parades: it helped emphasise the distance between themselves and the Weimar Republic.

Blaming socialists was hardly surprising for a deeply conservative officer class. It also appeared to be supported by the way the German socialist party, *Sozialdemokratische Partei Deutschlands* (SPD), took power in the Reichstag after the fall of the monarchy. However, this particular accusation gave the erroneous impression that the socialists, having opposed the war, were now climbing into power over the bodies of Germany's fallen soldiers. In fact, the SPD had split in early 1917 between those led by Friedrich Ebert, who supported the war and had voted the credits to finance it, and the more communist-influenced Spartacist League, led by Rosa Luxemburg and Karl Liebknecht, which opposed the war and whose leaders were imprisoned for their views. The truth was that military defeat left Germany facing revolution and chaos, and the Reichstag turned to the leader that it felt was best placed to balance the demands of the warring factions in the streets and of the Allies on the frontier, namely Ebert. Far from stabbing Germany, or even the Kaiser, in the back, Ebert had sought to retain the monarchy. He demanded full power for himself only when it was clear that the Kaiser was abdicating and that mutiny was spreading throughout the fleet and into the army. Ebert used his power to take robust military action against the communists: it was he who sent troops and *Freikorps* to crush the Spartacists. Nevertheless, Ebert's government was never able to escape the stigma of having accepted the Treaty of Versailles and, even worse, of having taken steps to ensure it was fulfilled.

The Paris Peace Conference and the Treaty of Versailles

Deep and bitter detestation of the Treaty of Versailles lay at the heart of Nazi foreign policy, so we need to have a good idea of why it took on such totemic significance for the Germans. Most attention is usually given, understandably enough, to the harsh terms the Allies imposed on Germany, which are sometimes compared with the equally harsh terms the Germans had imposed on the Russians only the year before at Brest-Litovsk. However, Versailles attained such symbolic significance in inter-war Germany precisely because it was, from start to finish, a symbolic exercise.

Usually the peace settlement at the end of a war is a limited affair between the combatants, perhaps with a third party acting as mediator, but the circumstances of 1919, with Europe in ruins and different ethnic groups in both Europe and the Middle East declaring independence and demanding their national territory, necessitated a much larger general settlement. The most obvious precedent was the Congress of Vienna (1814–15), which had redrawn the map of Europe at the end of the Napoleonic Wars almost exactly 100 years earlier. From the German point of view Vienna was a hopeful example. Napoleon had caused more widespread international disruption than the Kaiser had done, yet France had been treated relatively leniently in 1815. Most importantly, Vienna had been a congress, a summit meeting of representatives of sovereign states — including France — accorded equal status with each other. The Germans in 1919 had good reason to hope for similar treatment, especially given the conciliatory noises coming from the historically minded US President Wilson. Unfortunately for them, however, Wilson's view was not to prevail.

The impact of Woodrow Wilson

The important thing to remember when considering Woodrow Wilson is that in 1919 he was both older and much more ill than he appears in photographs. This helps explain both the breadth of his vision — this was his last chance to make a major impact on the world — and his weakness in not imposing his will on his allies. His decision to travel to Europe was a highly symbolic move. Europeans thought of America as a far-off land of opportunity, where people from any background might build a better life than was possible at home, but now the president of this fabled land was coming to Europe, armed with exciting new ideas for a better future.

Central to the aura surrounding Wilson's arrival in Europe were the boldness and imaginativeness of his peace proposals. Wilson was an academic historian by background and he had, or thought he had, a good understanding of Europe and its history. As a strict Protestant he also wanted to punish what he saw as the 'Godless Germans'. His Fourteen Points were a mixture of specific proposals for particular areas and of general principles that he believed would move the conduct of international politics onto a higher moral plane. The most celebrated example of these general principles was the proposal for a League of Nations, but the Points also called for complete freedom of navigation on the high seas (a long-standing bone of contention between the United States and Great Britain) and an end to secret diplomacy and alliances. Central to Wilson's thinking was the doctrine of national self-determination, according to which the different ethnic groupings of Europe were to be gathered in their own nation states. Wilson drew this idea from his reading of European history, according to which the tensions caused by the growth of supranational empires, such as the Austrian, Turkish and Russian, had led to the ethnic violence in the Balkans that had eventually triggered the Great War. His thinking was that, if the different European peoples' aspiration for independence were met, the main ground for European conflict would disappear.

Wilson's vision might have stood a better chance of general acceptance if the conference had been held in the United States with himself in the chair. The decision to hold it in Paris signalled that this was not to be a congress on the model of Vienna, with all parties treated equally, but a conference of the victors, which would impose a settlement on the defeated. The 1919 peacemakers believed that the Congress of Vienna had established the system of secret diplomacy and military alliances that led eventually to the Great War, and they were determined not to repeat what they perceived as their predecessors' mistakes. In practice, however, by deciding to ignore precedent and work to their own agenda, they handed complete control of proceedings to their hosts, and the French were the most bitterly and deeply anti-German of all the Allied powers.

Germany and the Treaty of Versailles

The Paris Peace Conference of 1919 was an odd affair. It did not have a central meeting hall where all delegates met. Instead, the 'Big Three' — Wilson, Lloyd George and Clemenceau — met in various hotel suites where they listened to presentations from different national delegations. Clemenceau revelled in his role as chairman, with Harold Nicolson, a member of the British delegation, comparing his peremptory style of chairmanship ('Any objections? Agreed') to a machine-gun. The Big Three would then retire to one of their hotel suites and chat over their brandy and cigars, sometimes crawling over a large map with pencils to see where the frontiers they had decided on would go, and rarely paying much attention to the economic experts in their entourages or to the detailed handbooks that had been prepared for their guidance. The whole conference had the feel of a gentlemen's club from which most of the delegates were excluded.

No one was more excluded than the German delegation. The French did everything possible to make them feel at a disadvantage. They arranged for them to travel to Paris by train through the devastated battlefields of northern France, the engine drivers slowing down so that delegates could get a good look. The Germans were lodged in the same hotel in Versailles where the French leaders had been placed in 1871 when they had to negotiate with the victorious Bismarck; they were made to carry their own luggage; and a guarded perimeter fence was set up around the hotel — officially for their own protection, but the impression was that they were imprisoned. The day for signing the treaty was set for 28 June, the anniversary of the assassination of the Archduke Franz Ferdinand in 1914, and the place was to be the Hall of Mirrors, on exactly the spot where the German empire had been proclaimed in 1871. The terms of the treaty were communicated to the German delegation in advance with a clear indication that they were non-negotiable and that, if the German government did not sign, the Allies would resume the war and invade Germany. The German foreign minister Count Ulrich von Brockdorff-Rantzau, a pompous old-school diplomat who made a bad impression on the Allied representatives by inter-rupting Clemenceau and making an overlong speech of protest at Germany's treatment, resigned rather than sign what he considered a dishonourable peace. The Germans had to send his newly appointed replacement, Hermann Müller, and the transport minister, the only other member of the government who would agree to go.

This is not the place to consider the detailed provisions of the Treaty of Versailles; what matters is how the Germans responded to them. Versailles was not the first draconian peace settlement in history, yet both it and the treaties imposed on Germany's allies, Hungary and Turkey, occasioned unusually deep bitterness. German schoolchildren had special lessons in the injustice of the Treaty of Versailles, and those politicians who had agreed to accept it were branded 'November criminals'. Some terms were grudgingly accepted. For example, no German government made recovery of Germany's overseas colonies a priority. Similarly, the losses of Alsace-Lorraine to France and Eupen-Malmédy to Belgium were generally accepted as the price of defeat. The land losses in the east caused much more outrage, partly because they were so much larger and cut through the original heartland of Prussia, but also because of the countries that would benefit. The Poles and Lithuanians had been Germany's great enemies in the past: the Teutonic knights had led crusades against the pagan Lithuanians in the Middle Ages. Poland had disappeared from the map in the eighteenth century, carved up by its neighbours: Austria, Russia and Prussia; many Germans could not see why a nation that had not even been able to free itself should be given large tracts of ethnic German land.

The Germans were equally unimpressed by the other 'successor states' set up by the ethnic groups that had been part of the old Austro–Hungarian empire. Giving 'lesser' nations, such as the Czechs or the Croats, their own nation states seemed perverse to many Germans, especially since the sheer artificiality of these states seemed to be indicated by their cumbersome names, Czechoslovakia and the Kingdom of Serbs, Croats and Slovenes (which was considered such a mouthful that it changed to 'Yugoslavia' a few years later). The fact that these different ethnic groups, some of them deadly rivals, were allowed to band together in new states while the Austrians and Germans, ethnically identical, were forbidden to do so seemed to indicate the hollowness of Wilson's doctrine of national self-determination.

Key to the Germans' anger over Versailles was what they saw as a hypocritical claim that the treaty was based on a higher set of moral values. The idea that a war could be *blamed* on someone was a novelty in diplomacy, which seemed to the Germans to be flying in the face of reality. They were speechless when they learned of the corollary of the 'war-guilt clause': reparations. Imposing an obligation on a defeated country to indemnify the victors was far from new: the Germans had done it to France in 1871 and kept an army of occupation in the country until it was paid. Reparations, however, imposed an open-ended duty on the defeated country to recompense the victims for the damage the war had caused. How this sum was to be calculated, who qualified as a victim, what counted as war damage, how much the payments were to be, how long they were to be made — all these questions were left unanswered. Reparations effectively gave the Allies, principally the French, the right to help themselves to Germany's national bank account for the foreseeable future.

Everything about Versailles, including its terms and the circumstances in which it was signed, suggested that the Allies were not recognising Germany as a sovereign state on a par with their own. Indeed, the Allies did not accept Germany as an equal: they saw it as the embodiment of militarism. The terms of the treaty were harsh not just in order to placate French and British calls for revenge but also to eradicate the means and mentality for war from the Germans' minds, to help keep the world at peace and safe for democracy. The Treaty of Versailles represented the Allies not only at their most vengeful but also at their most high-minded and moral. That was why successive German governments sought not only to get particular aspects of the Treaty of Versailles reversed but also to destroy the philosophy that underpinned it.

Questions

1 Why did Germans find it so difficult to accept the reality of defeat in November 1918?

2 To what extent did Nazi foreign policy grow out of the events of the First World War?

3 'The real fault of the Treaty of Versailles was not that it punished Germany too harshly, but that it was not nearly harsh enough.' How far do you agree with this opinion?

The foreign policy of the Weimar Republic

One of the most hotly debated issues about Nazi foreign policy is the extent to which it followed that of the Weimar Republic. The Nazis openly campaigned against the Weimar governments' policy of fulfilling the Treaty of Versailles, but how accurate was their claim to be setting a different course in foreign policy from that of the despised republic and the 'November criminals'?

The new republic had to face up to the fact that many Germans would never accept it, no matter what it achieved. Die-hard monarchists could never forgive the socialists who dominated the new republic for forcing the Kaiser to abdicate; the fact that the Allies would undoubtedly have done the same did not affect their attitude. More radical socialists and communists could never forgive the republic for the fate of the Spartacists. The army, which detested civilian rule in any case, was delighted to allow the republic to bear the blame for its own failure to win the war. However, by far the greatest complaint Germans had against their new republic was the fact that it accepted the Treaty of Versailles and encouraged them to fulfil its humiliating terms. Few Germans realised, or cared, that if the republic had refused to sign the treaty the Allies would have resumed the war and imposed even worse terms. So bitter was the anger against those politicians who had accepted Versailles that two of them, the former finance minister Matthias Erzberger and the foreign minister Walther Rathenau, both advocates of the policy of fulfilment of the treaty's terms, were assassinated. We must begin, therefore, by looking at the impact of Versailles on Weimar's conduct of foreign policy.

The impact of Versailles

From the moment the treaty was signed it was clear that the German government had little room for manoeuvre. It was all very well Germans speaking of the 'November criminals' who had signed the treaty and talking airily of tearing the thing up, but the reality of the situation made such a policy impossible. The failure of Weimar politicians to communicate this simple message to the German people, or perhaps the wilful refusal of the Germans to recognise it, constitutes the Weimar Republic's most serious, and ultimately fatal, weakness. As long as Germany's governments did not explicitly reject Versailles and refuse to comply with it, it did not matter how many deals it struck, nor how advantageous they might be to Germany: the German people would not be satisfied.

Weimar Germany and Bolshevik Russia

The country to which the government of Weimar Germany turned first was not one of the western powers but Russia. This can come as a surprise to students, but it was part of a pattern of German diplomatic overtures to Russia, which long predated both Weimar and the Russian Revolution. Germans dated the emergence of their sense of nationhood to Napoleon's disastrous retreat from Moscow in 1812, counting the action they took then against the retreating French as their first truly national rising. Bismarck, who had served as ambassador in St Petersburg, made good relations with Russia a priority for the newly united Germany in the 1870s. By the 1890s, however, the situation had changed and the German general staff were planning for war with Russia. The Schlieffen Plan was designed to eliminate France quickly precisely because the Germans realised just how vast an undertaking the invasion of Russia would be.

The experience of the Great War and of the Russian Revolution did not change this generally positive German attitude towards Russia quite as much as one might expect. The reason the Germans imposed such harsh terms on the Bolshevik government at Brest-Litovsk in 1918 was because they believed that such an opportunity to weaken the Russians was not likely to recur. Sure enough, Trotsky's success in forging the Red Army into a formidable fighting force and seeing off the White and Allied armies was a sign that Russia would soon be on its military feet again. Nor was Russia's Bolshevism an insuperable barrier to good relations with Germany in peacetime. To some extent diplomats always have to hold their noses and deal with regimes they thoroughly dislike, and the Germans certainly disliked Bolshevism. In 1918 the entire staff of the Russian embassy in Berlin was deported for helping the German communists foment revolution. However, in the 1920s Germany and Russia had a lot in common: they were both regarded as potential threats to the peace and stability of Europe, shunned by the other powers and forbidden to join the League of Nations. Both countries hated the Treaty of Versailles. The Russians resented not having been involved in the negotiations at Paris and were angry that the Allies had recognised the Baltic States, Estonia, Latvia and Lithuania, which had shaken off Russian rule. They were even more angry that the Treaty of Versailles had established an independent Poland. The Polish delegation in Paris had laid claim to vast areas of Russian territory in Ukraine and in 1920 they had taken advantage of the chaos in Russia to send troops in to seize it. The Russians had invited the Germans to join them in the war to cut Poland down to size, and although political reality made it impossible for Germany to accept the offer, the incident showed that Bolshevik Moscow was open to links with Berlin. It was not long before those links were forged.

The Treaty of Rapallo

Some figures within the German government, including General von Seeckt, head of the army, and von Brockdorff-Rantzau, the foreign minister-turned-ambassador to Moscow, shared a strong, if sentimental, vision of a mystic union of Teuton (German) and Slav, and lobbied heavily for a formal German–Russian alliance. The new foreign minister appointed in 1922, Walther Rathenau, was another believer and in April 1922 he slipped away from an international economic conference being held at Genoa to meet up with his Soviet counterpart, Georgy Chicherin, at Rapallo, a small town 20 miles down the coast. There the two men signed the Treaty of Rapallo, one of the most curious but significant acts of Weimar's foreign policy.

Under the terms of Rapallo, both states renounced their territorial and financial claims on each other. This drew a line under the legacy of the Great War and Brest-Litovsk. It also freed their hands to work in partnership to deal with Poland. In this sense, Rapallo was a direct forerunner of the Nazi–Soviet Pact. The treaty also established mutually beneficial trading arrangements at a time when the rest of the world was extremely wary of establishing trade relations with the Soviet Union and Germany's economic ties with the west were skewed by the need to meet its reparations targets. The most important aspect of Rapallo, however, was its secret annex, by which the Russians provided the Germans with military training facilities in return for German help to modernise the Red Army. The German military aviation firm Junkers and the Krupp arms-manufacturing corporation both established plants in Russia and the Germans were also able to set up a military flying school, a tank school and a chemical weapons facility deep in Russian territory, well away from the prying eyes of Allied weapons inspectors. The Rapallo agreement was extended in November 1922 to cover all the non-Russian republics within the Soviet Union. By then, a change of personnel was under way in Berlin: the pro-Russian Rathenau was assassinated on 24 June 1922 and in 1923 the French invasion of the Ruhr and the Great Inflation that followed brought Gustav Stresemann into power as chancellor.

Stresemann did not share Rathenau's vision of a German–Russian alliance and sought instead to develop closer relations with the western powers. This alarmed Moscow, which saw them as hostile. The closer Stresemann drew to the British and French, the more the Russians, strongly supported by von Brockdorff-Rantzau, tried to tempt him back with the offer of a partition of Poland. Stresemann was far too realistic to accept this offer, but he could not afford to alienate the pro-Russia lobby either, especially the powerful figure of General von Seeckt. So when he got Germany into the League of Nations in 1926 Stresemann sweetened the pill for the Russians with the Treaty of Berlin, which confirmed the terms agreed at Rapallo and guaranteed each side's neutrality for a period of 5 years. Moreover, Stresemann did not rule out a Russo–German partition of Poland at some point. The Treaty of Berlin was widely interpreted as a thinly veiled threat to Poland, especially when the extent of German military training in Russia was revealed by a report in a British newspaper, *The Manchester Guardian*. The western allies, especially the British, were henceforth concerned to woo Germany away from Russia; if the price was a general loosening of the terms of Versailles, for example by withdrawing Allied occupation forces from the country, they were quite prepared to pay it.

The foreign policy of Gustav Stresemann

Stresemann has benefited more than any other Weimar statesman from comparisons with Hitler. He was sometimes referred to in English-speaking countries as a 'good German', as if that made him a rarity. Stresemann began in the National Liberal Party (*Nationalliberale Partei*), of which he was elected leader in 1917. The National Liberals had always stood for parliamentary government, but they had also long had a soft spot for the military. In the 1860s and 1870s the National Liberals had swallowed their liberal principles and supported Bismarck's authoritarian regime; many had been enthusiastic supporters of colonial expansion. In particular, the National Liberals had always been firm believers in the absolute integrity of Germany's historic lands. In 1848, when they briefly seized power and set up a national parliament in Frankfurt, they promptly embarked on a war with Denmark to regain the 'lost' provinces of Schleswig and Holstein and then demanded a further war to force Bohemia (the modern-day Czech Republic) into Germany, maintaining that the Czechs were a Germanic people with no need of a separate state of their own, which was more or less what the Nazis said about them in the 1930s.

As a liberal, therefore, Stresemann was already broadly in sympathy with the expansionist foreign policy of imperial Germany before 1914. The experience of the Great War served only to make him even more right wing, much as it did for Mussolini and Hitler. Stresemann became such an ardent supporter of German expansion, not to mention of unrestricted U-boat warfare, that he became an embarrassment to his own party and had to leave it in 1919 to set up his own German People's Party (*Deutsche Volkspartei* or DVP), which consisted of right-wing liberals like himself. In its support for traditional family values and opposition to high tariffs, government subsidies and benefit payments, the DVP was essentially an old-style conservative party. Initially it was cool towards the Weimar Republic. Like the army, it stood by during the 1920 right-wing Kapp Putsch, when the government had to call a general strike to defeat the putschists. However, once it was clear that the republic would survive the crises it faced in its early years, Stresemann came round to the idea of supporting it in order to achieve his more ambitious aims. Here, too, he had something in common with Hitler.

It is of crucial significance that it was Stresemann himself who extricated the Weimar Republic from its most serious crisis of all, the Great Inflation of 1923. This inflation was one of the most traumatic peacetime experiences Germany went through in the twentieth century, and for the rest of the century it left Germans with a deeply ingrained sensitivity about the value of their money. Great importance was attached to the value of western-backed currency when Germany was divided after 1945, and again when it was reunited in 1990. Memories of 1923 were also behind the caution with which Germans accepted the loss of the Deutschmark in favour of the euro in 2002.

The inflation was sparked by a chain of events beginning with the decision by Chancellor Wilhelm Cuno to suspend reparations payments in protest at what he saw as an unreasonable French demand for increased rates. The suspension was in direct defiance of the Treaty of Versailles, and it prompted the French and Belgian invasion and occupation of the Ruhr to ensure the treaty was upheld. The occupation, although bitterly resented in Germany and disapproved of by the British and Americans, was in line with the terms of the treaty; the German response, to call a general strike in the Ruhr and thus paralyse the entire German economy, was therefore in defiance of the treaty. Standing up to the French won Cuno some short-term political popularity, but only at the expense of the inflation. To Stresemann, the lesson of the events of 1923 could hardly have been clearer: simply to defy Versailles and ignore its provisions, however popular such a move might be in Germany, was to court disaster. The treaty would have to be defeated — for such was definitely Stresemann's aim — by working within its provisions.

The most obvious issue to deal with first was reparations. Their imposition was justified by the war-guilt clause, which many Germans felt to be the single most unjust aspect of the whole treaty. As long as the Allies could demand reparations payments at will, Germany could never be regarded as an equal partner in Europe with France and Britain. Equally, the more Germany was accepted as an equal, the harder it would be for the Allies to insist on full payment of reparations. The invasion of the Ruhr had shown that it was unrealistic to hope for a change of heart on the Allied side; however, lightening the reparations burden might be feasible. In the event, Stresemann did better than that. The 1924 Dawes Plan, brokered by the American financier Charles Dawes, acting on behalf of the American government, laid down a regular and manageable schedule for Germany's reparations payments: no more could the French simply demand more from Germany whenever they felt like it. Moreover, the Allies agreed never again to take unilateral military action to enforce the treaty, as the French and Belgians had done in the Ruhr. In future all parties would have to agree to any such action, which was highly unlikely to happen, given that Britain had been fiercely critical of the course taken by the French and was looking for ways to lighten Versailles' grip on Germany. By any reasonable estimation, the Dawes Plan was a major defeat for the French and a diplomatic coup for Germany.

Reactions in Germany to the Dawes Plan, however, illustrated the difficulties Stresemann was up against. Far from greeting the plan as a diplomatic triumph, Germans were dismayed that Stresemann had not got the treaty rescinded. Accepting even a modified form of reparations payments was seen as surrender to the single most odious feature of Versailles. Moreover, even though reparations payments were now to be regular, there was still no end-date envisaged until almost the end of the century, a prospect that filled Germans with angry despair. Stresemann found himself accused of being a stooge for the allies; Ludendorff went further and called the Dawes Plan a 'Jewish Tannenberg' — in other words a catastrophic defeat. Stresemann had to take these accusations seriously. Rathenau, himself Jewish, had been gunned down by two right-wing army officers outraged by his policy of fulfilling the terms of the hated treaty and by his diplomatic overtures to Moscow. As if to prove the critics' point, the Allies' control commission cancelled the planned military evacuation of Cologne in protest at the widespread evasion of the military terms of Versailles that their officers were reporting. It seemed that the Dawes Plan had extended the Allied occupation, not shortened it.

The Locarno Conference

The League of Nations was both the most hopeful and the most frustrating legacy of President Wilson's impact on world affairs. The idea of a world government devoted to the cause of peace was difficult to argue against, but the covenant of the League was lacking in detail and riddled with anomalies. The United States' self-imposed exclusion from the League looked bizarre, but at least it was the result of a decision of the US Congress. Germany and the Soviet Union were banned from the League, in flat contradiction of the principles the covenant was supposed to enshrine. The council of the League had four permanent members, Britain, France, Italy and Japan, all of them wartime allies. Other countries, such as Spain, Brazil and the newly independent Poland, did not see why they, too, should not sit permanently on the council. The way the covenant had been written into the peace treaties in 1919 and imposed on the defeated powers, as if a world government dedicated to world peace were some sort of punishment, was also increasingly looking like a misjudgement. By 1924, the idea was growing that it might be time to gather the major powers together to look more systematically at the League and at European territorial arrangements. If he handled it carefully, Stresemann could seize this opportunity to start undermining the territorial clauses of the Treaty of Versailles.

Key to Stresemann's calculations was the strained relationship between Britain and France. The British had been critical of the French occupation of the Ruhr and the French resented it, feeling that they had been let down by the perfidious English. The British had always been uneasy about the Treaty of Versailles anyway. Lloyd George had disliked the vindictive attitude the French had adopted at Paris in 1919, and the most scathing attack on the treaty's provisions had come from the Cambridge economist John Maynard Keynes, who compared it to the 'peace' the Romans had imposed on Carthage, i.e. destroying it completely. The Dawes Plan, which amounted to a rebuke to the French for taking such an aggressive line towards the Germans, had been largely the work of the British Labour Prime Minister Ramsay MacDonald.

If Stresemann could somehow drive a wedge between the British and French, he might be able to win the advantage and make progress towards revising Germany's borders. Unfortunately for him, in 1924 the Conservatives returned to power in Britain under Stanley Baldwin, who appointed Austen Chamberlain foreign secretary. Chamberlain (elder brother to Neville Chamberlain and not to be confused with him) was strongly pro-French and could be expected to heal some of the bitterness the French felt after the Ruhr invasion. If Stresemann wanted to separate Britain from France he would have to make his move fast.

Stresemann's approach, when it came, was not to the British but to the French. In 1925 he gathered the countries with territory along the Rhine to sign a Rhineland Pact, agreeing not to use force to settle any disputes they might have. Under the pact Germany accepted the Rhine frontier, which meant giving up any idea of retrieving Alsace and Lorraine, and also accepted that the German Rhineland should remain a demilitarised zone. Britain and Italy both signed the pact as guarantors. Had these countries all been in the League of Nations, such an agreement would not have been necessary; the obvious conclusion was that Germany ought to be admitted to the League, and negotiations began to arrange just that. Since the reason Germany had not been allowed into the League was its supposed guilt for the war, this move in itself weakened the central pillar of the Treaty of Versailles. Stresemann pressed home his advantage by insisting that Germany be exempted from the military obligations that membership of the League involved; it was easy to argue a special case because of the limitations the Treaty of Versailles imposed on the size of the German armed forces. (Contrary to popular misconception, the League of Nations did have the option to deploy military forces. However, since the decision to use them had to be unanimous, the chances of their ever being deployed were remote.) The French thought Germany should accept the same terms as everyone else, but Stresemann held out for the exemption, reckoning, rightly, that the British and French would rather concede the point than risk the talks failing. He got his way.

Ironing out the anomalies

Stresemann took the opportunity of the Rhineland Pact to start raising the issue of a general settlement of European issues, to iron out the anomalies left by the 1919 treaties. Chamberlain was open to the idea. If the French were a bit more hesitant, it was because they could see that they had most to gain from maintaining the status quo and most to lose from any change; they were also aware that no one stood to gain more from a general settlement than Germany. The fact that Stresemann persuaded the powers to agree to a settlement was due in no small part to personal factors. He had a genial manner and got on well with both Chamberlain and Aristide Briand, the socialist French foreign minister. They settled on a venue in neutral Switzerland at Locarno, just across Lake Maggiore from Italy so that Mussolini, who neither particularly wanted to join in the detailed discussions, nor cared to be left out of them, could drop in and out of the conference by speedboat.

Agreeing Germany's western borders was relatively easy, especially after the Rhineland Pact; however, Stresemann also successfully stalled French demands that Germany offer a similar guarantee of its eastern borders. The fact that the conference ended without agreement on these meant not only that Germany would want to revisit the issue at a later date but also that the Locarno powers, by clear implication, supported its right to do so. When one considers the low point from which Stresemann had started in 1923, with Germany occupied, humiliated and in economic meltdown, the progress he had made towards restoring its international standing and making inroads on Versailles was remarkable. In 1926 Germany got the reward Stresemann had pressed for by being admitted into the League of Nations, welcomed by Aristide Briand in an emotional ceremony of Franco–German reconciliation in the League's General Assembly Hall in Geneva. The two men crowned the achievements of the remarkable years 1925–26 by jointly winning the Nobel Peace Prize.

With hindsight one can identify 1926 as the pinnacle of Stresemann's career, but his campaign to wear down the Allies' insistence on the terms of Versailles did not stop there. He cannily played on British and French fears of the Soviet Union, and shortly after the ceremony in Geneva signed the Treaty of Berlin with the Soviet Union, confirming the terms of the Treaty of Rapallo. This was followed by *The Manchester Guardian*'s revelations about the extent of German military training in Russia. Stresemann was gently reminding the western Allies how much they depended on German goodwill; as a result, the Allies started a phased withdrawal of their occupation troops from the Rhineland, and the French agreed to evacuate the whole zone by 1930. Stresemann was aware that the French would take any opportunity to go back on this undertaking and that he needed to maintain the moral pressure on the Allies to loosen their grip on the country. The result was the 1929 Young Plan, an agreement on reparations payments negotiated by diplomat Owen D. Young, which revised the 1924 Dawes Plan, rescheduling the payments, steadily reducing the amount Germany had to pay and for the first time laying down an agreed end date for the whole process: 1988. In return, Stresemann extracted from the French a definite commitment to withdraw their last occupation forces from the Rhineland by 1930 at the latest.

Most students, learning of the Young Plan, picture it in much the same way that the Germans saw it at the time, as a pattern of relentless payments, year after year, generation after generation, until a date that only children alive in 1929 could hope to see. However, if Stresemann had shown one thing in his years as foreign minister, it was that these agreements with the Allies did not need to be as firm as they looked. Without ever defying the Treaty of Versailles, Stresemann had started, clause by clause, to dilute it, not against the Allies' opposition but with their wholehearted agreement. He had got them to accept that the territorial settlement of Versailles should not be regarded as permanent but was open to further negotiation; he had persuaded them to rescind the ban on Germany joining the League of Nations; he had induced them, in effect, to renounce the use of force to uphold the treaty; and even the revelations about Germany getting round the treaty by training military personnel in Russia had not prompted the Allies to take military action. Above all, he coaxed the Allies into recognising that, as to reparations, neither Versailles nor the Dawes Plan was to be regarded as final. As long as the German foreign ministry kept its head, the Young Plan, too, could no doubt be renegotiated in due course, to Germany's advantage. In short, Stresemann had largely achieved what had seemed very far off when he took office in 1923: the restoration of Germany's international status and independent freedom of action.

German reactions to Stresemann

Put like this, it is difficult to see what there was for Germans not to like in Stresemann's policy. Yet the truth is that he faced opposition from a wide range of political groups including the Nationalists, the Communists and the Nazis. On the right, the Nationalists and the much less significant Nazis denounced Stresemann for not simply tearing the treaty up. The Young Plan was denounced in such fierce terms that it might have been a second Treaty of Versailles. Hugenberg, the Nationalist leader, even introduced a bill into the Reichstag, which would have made adherence to the terms of Versailles a treasonable offence. On the left, the Communists, taking orders directly from Moscow, saw Stresemann as the poodle of the capitalist powers, Britain and France, and denounced the League of Nations as an anti-Soviet front. Attacked from both sides, Stresemann had to rely on the moderate socialists and the Catholic Centre Party for support. He was both losing friends and gaining enemies.

General von Seeckt, who, despite his initial lack of enthusiasm for the Weimar Republic and his dreams of an alliance with Russia, had become an important source of support to Stresemann, was forced to resign after he allowed the Kaiser's grandson to attend a military review in breach of the law excluding the imperial family from public life. Meanwhile the nationalist movement was growing in confidence. The old ramshackle *Freikorps* had largely been replaced by the more organised *Stahlhelm*, a large and highly trained paramilitary force that took a leading role in stirring up opposition to the Young Plan. In 1927 President von Hindenburg, speaking at a dedication ceremony to those who had died at the Battle of Tannenberg, denied that Germany had been to blame for the Great War, a statement that went directly against the policy of his own foreign minister and indicated how high up frustration with Stresemann had reached. Stresemann desperately needed to gather a strong political coalition behind him if he was to keep up the pressure on the Allies to withdraw their troops from German soil, and the last months of his life were devoted to trying to put just such a coalition together. In the end his health, never good, gave way under the strain and he succumbed to a heart attack on 3 October 1929. Three weeks later, the Wall Street Crash brought the American economy, on which Germany's prosperity depended, grinding to a halt.

The final years of Weimar

The full extent to which German economic fortunes depended on American investment was revealed when the American economy collapsed in the aftermath of the Wall Street Crash. The collapse hit Germany in two ways. First, American investment, which had been of bonanza proportions while Germany needed help rebuilding in the 1920s, suddenly dried up, to be replaced by peremptory American demands for repayment of loans. German companies and town corporations simply could not meet this sudden demand for money. Second, the US Congress responded to the crash by passing a prohibitive set of tariffs, which had the effect of closing the United States to imports. Other countries responded with tariffs of their own, so that within a few months of the crash world trade had virtually dried up. This hit manufacturing across Europe and produced the chronic unemployment that was such a feature of the Depression. The British and French attempted to work their way out of the crisis by exploiting the economic potential of their overseas empires. No such possibility was open to Germany, and when in 1931 the Germans raised the idea of a customs union with Austria to help both countries weather the storm, the French, suddenly keen again to enforce the Treaty of Versailles, forbade it.

For Germany the worst year of the crisis was 1931 because that was when the Austrian bank Credit Anstalt collapsed, followed by the German Darmstadt and National Bank, prompting a run on the banks throughout Germany and a credit crunch across the continent. Faced with financial meltdown for the second time in a decade, Chancellor Heinrich Brüning, who had come to power in 1930 with support from General von Schleicher and the army, turned desperately to foreign governments for help. US President Hoover, an old friend of Stresemann who knew something about relieving hardship in Europe, having organised famine relief for refugees after the Great War, proposed a 1-year moratorium on German reparations payments. In 1932 an international conference at Lausanne effectively postponed further reparations indefinitely. These moves were certainly welcome news for Germany, but they had little immediate impact on the plight of Germany's ever-growing army of unemployed.

At the height of the economic crisis the Treaty of Versailles had one last, somewhat ironic, blow to deliver to Germany's hopes of recovery. Although the treaty's limitations on the German armed forces had been enforced, nothing much had been done about the more general commitment to disarmament made at the Paris Peace Conference. In 1928 Aristide Briand and the US Secretary of State, Frank B. Kellogg, drew up a pact renouncing war, which all the major powers signed, but since it contained no provision for punishing those who broke it the Kellogg–Briand Pact was little more than a set of fine words. Now, at the height of the world economic crisis, the League of Nations turned to the issue and set up an international Disarmament Conference, which convened at Geneva in 1932. Had the economic situation been brighter, the Germans might have felt some satisfaction that the other powers were coming round to the sort of disarmament they had forced on Germany at Versailles but, as it was, if the conference did impose swingeing measures of disarmament, it would mean even worse news for German heavy industry. When Hitler came to power in 1933, after the complex political manoeuvring of the previous year, one of the first things he did was to withdraw from the Disarmament Conference. It is not hard to see why the move was so well received by the German people. It seemed to symbolise a new sense of national confidence and a more decisive approach to foreign policy; in reality, it was in line with the logic underlying German foreign policy for most of the Weimar years.

Questions

1 Explain why the Treaty of Versailles had such an impact on the foreign policy of Weimar Germany.
2 To what extent did Gustav Stresemann deserve to be known as the 'good German'?
3 How successful was the foreign policy of Weimar Germany in the period 1919–29?

Nazi foreign policy, phase one: rearmament, 1933–36

Foreign policy was central to Nazism. It is difficult to conceive of a Nazi movement arising in Germany without the Treaty of Versailles to kick against; *Lebensraum* was a foreign-policy issue, and even the war against the Jews was thought of in global terms. Yet when they came into office the Nazis had little knowledge of foreign affairs and no consistent plan of how they might achieve their vision for Germany's future; they had to negotiate a steep learning curve. As a result, their foreign policy fell into three distinct phases. In the first phase, which lasted from 1933 to the remilitarisation of the Rhineland in 1936, most attention was given to establishing the Nazi dictatorship at home, and foreign policy was largely devoted to clearing the way for Germany to rearm. The second phase, from 1936 to 1938, saw the Nazis give priority to foreign policy, challenging the western powers and carrying out territorial annexations in Austria and Czechoslovakia. The third phase, from 1938–39, saw a more aggressive policy, from the invasion of the rump of Czechoslovakia and of Memel to the full-scale invasion of Poland. This chapter deals with the first phase. The second and third will be the subjects of Chapters 6 and 7.

Mein Kampf and *Lebensraum*

The principal source for anyone wanting to grasp the Nazi outlook on the rest of the world is Hitler's *Mein Kampf*, his political testament written in Landsberg prison after the failure of the Munich Putsch of 1923. *Mein Kampf* is a difficult book to interpret, not helped by its rambling and repetitive style.

A passage where Hitler identifies Russia and its vassal states as the area needed for Germany's *Lebensraum* is often seized on as evidence of his long-term foreign policy aims, but it does not follow from this that he was planning or even contemplating an invasion of the Soviet Union from 1924 onwards. The concept of *Lebensraum* was not unique to Hitler; it was a common feature of

German nationalist writings. Nor was the identification of Russia as Germany's promised land particularly original. Where else could it be? Not even Hitler pretended Germany had any right to France or Italy, and Germans had long rejected the idea of absorbing the non-German lands of the old Habsburg Empire. In any case, these areas were fully settled and industrially advanced. Russia, on the other hand, had vast open spaces that in the 1920s and 1930s were still relatively undeveloped. If Germany was going to have *Lebensraum*, it was fairly obvious it would have to be in Russia.

What was new about *Mein Kampf*'s case was Hitler's injection into the argument of a major strand of anti-Semitism and anti-Bolshevism. Just as the nineteenth-century American journalist Horace Greeley had described the Native American tribes as 'children' who did not deserve to hold on to vast tracts of lands they did not know how to exploit properly, so the Russians, through their backwardness and by providing a base for the 'Jewish–Bolshevik conspiracy' against western civilisation, had, Hitler claimed, forfeited the right to hold on to the valuable land they occupied. It was Germany's manifest destiny to take it from them.

How seriously should we take *Mein Kampf*? Knowing what we do about subsequent events, we can scarcely dismiss it out of hand. The terrible work of the wartime *Einsatzgruppen* in clearing Russian territory, massacring its inhabitants and destroying their homes, as well as the policy of gassing the Jewish population of Europe in the death camps, shows that Hitler's sweeping rhetoric was deadly serious. However, although *Mein Kampf* may be good evidence of Hitler's general aims, it is unreliable evidence of *policy*. The book did not envisage the Germans going to war with their ethnic cousins, the Anglo-Saxon English, for example, nor was there any hint of the Germans making common cause with the Japanese. Without further corroboration, *Mein Kampf* cannot be taken as firm evidence of Hitler's detailed intentions.

Who ran Nazi foreign policy?

The foreign service of the NSDAP was led by the self-styled Nazi Party philosopher, Alfred Rosenberg, author of a shallow and pretentious work called *The Myth of the Twentieth Century*. In 1933 he was placed in charge of the party's foreign policy office, the *Aussenpolitische Amt*, but proved completely ineffective. Instead, Hitler relied on the existing German foreign ministry, which, like foreign ministries across Europe, was staffed by old-school civil servants and diplomats, conservative in temperament and naturally inclined towards negotiating their way through difficulties by talking with their like-minded counterparts in the foreign ministries of other countries. Indeed, the fact that Hitler was prepared to use the un-Nazified foreign ministry was a reflection of his political weakness in 1933. Hitler was head of a coalition government in which the Nazis were a minority. President Hindenburg insisted on Hitler's retaining Baron Constantin von Neurath as foreign minister. An aristocrat from the traditional school of German diplomacy, von Neurath proved highly capable, guiding Hitler skilfully through the rocky period of the early 1930s, withdrawing Germany from the Geneva Disarmament Conference and the League of Nations while still retaining international respect, and extricating Germany from the disastrous *putsch* attempt in Austria in 1934. However, as Hitler gained in confidence in his foreign dealings through the later 1930s, von Neurath found himself having to compete for influence with other figures, most notably Hermann Goering and Joachim von Ribbentrop, who all pursued their own foreign policy initiatives independently of the foreign ministry. The ministry itself was split between 'Ostlers', who favoured close relations with Russia, and 'Westlers', including von Neurath, who favoured better relations with the west. It is therefore difficult to say with absolute certainty what Nazi foreign policy was at any given point, or who ran it.

Some party members, especially those who had come to Nazism from other nationalist parties, wanted a restoration of Germany's pre-1914 frontiers, a strong navy and a tough line with the traditional enemy, England. Some even wanted the Kaiser back. More radically minded members, many of them in the SA or followers of the Strasser brothers, wanted to preach liberation to the colonial peoples of the British and French empires (although some of them also wanted to take land in Africa for German *Lebensraum*); this went directly against Hitler's support for the British empire, and little was heard of this school of thinking after the Night of the Long Knives in 1934. Better attuned to Hitler's way of thinking was the 'Blood and Soil' group under agriculture minister Darré, which believed Germany should avoid colonial adventures and instead seek to purify itself by settling the 'virgin lands' in Russia, although it had few practical suggestions for how to do it.

Outside the party, the main group with an influence on foreign policy was the military. The war minister, General von Blomberg, disliked the Nazis but approved of rearmament, not least because it would strengthen the army at the expense of the despised SA. Many generals viewed the Nazis' attacks on Jewish war veterans and airy talk of war with considerable distaste; it is no coincidence that leading figures within the army drew up secret plans to overthrow Hitler. Goering's *Luftwaffe*, by contrast, was much more Nazi in outlook. Its very existence depended on Hitler's defying the Treaty of Versailles and it was accordingly loyal to him. The navy under Admiral Erich Raeder was perhaps the most traditional in its outlook. Raeder thought in traditional terms of expanding the navy to challenge Britain.

Hitler, who had too much respect for British power to provoke it unnecessarily, only occasionally allowed policy to be driven by naval priorities.

Lastly, foreign policy was often driven by Hitler himself. He enjoyed meeting leaders face to face, and the annexations of 1938–39 were all preceded by a summons to the other countries' leaders to meet the Führer at one of his mountain-top retreats where Hitler enjoyed alternating charm and official protocol with furious harangues and overt intimidation, sometimes upping the stakes or changing his mind without warning. This confused picture of the running of foreign policy in Nazi Germany helps explain why western leaders, while viewing Hitler himself with distaste or alarm, were nevertheless willing to negotiate with him, thinking that more reasonable or rational figures within the German government might be able to exercise a calming influence over policy.

Agreements with the Pope and the Poles, 1933–34

Historians have pointed out the close relationship between Nazi foreign and domestic policy. Nowhere was this better illustrated than in the new regime's first diplomatic agreement, the Concordat with the Vatican negotiated with the papal nuncio to Germany, Cardinal Pacelli, by the devoutly Catholic von Papen. An accord with the Catholic Church lent Hitler an image of respectability and made him look more successful even than Bismarck, who had engaged in a bitter but ultimately futile feud with the Vatican. The Concordat was a straight political deal: the German government promised to safeguard the position of the Catholic Church within Germany, especially its schools and youth groups; in return the Church instructed the Catholic clergy and other Catholic groups to keep out of German politics.

Germany's other diplomatic move in these early months was a 10-year non-aggression pact signed with Poland in January 1934. Poland was a deeply Catholic state, almost as anti-communist and anti-Semitic as the Nazis themselves. Moreover, it had held its own against Trotsky's Red Army in the Russo–Polish War of 1919–20 and was still led by the grizzled old hero of that war, Marshal Pilsudski. Pilsudski declared in March 1933 that he would fight rather than allow Poland's borders to be altered and, since Poland's armed forces in 1934 were something like twice the size of Germany's, this threat of pre-emptive action had to be taken seriously. The pact removed the immediate threat and left Hitler free to build up his armed forces without having to worry about his eastern frontier.

Withdrawal from the League

Getting Germany accepted into the League of Nations had been one of Stresemann's greatest achievements and the German foreign ministry was in no hurry to squander it. Von Blomberg detested the League in principle, and he was particularly vehement against it in 1933 because it had set up a major Disarmament Conference the previous year to agree arms reductions in all member states. Von Blomberg, who was pressing for expansion of the army in order to counter-balance Ernst Roehm's over-mighty SA, urged Hitler to ignore the foreign ministry and withdraw from both the League and the conference. Hitler agreed, but where von Blomberg had thought in terms of Germany storming angrily from the conference hall, as Japan did in 1933, Hitler's approach was much more subtle.

The Disarmament Conference had run into problems from the moment it opened in 1932 because the French had insisted on full implementation of the disarmament terms of the Treaty of Versailles. Chancellor Brüning, badly needing a foreign policy success to boost his political position at home, proposed a cut in the period of service in the German army, but this had been rejected by the French, who wanted a general European settlement with definite military guarantees of their security. By the time the conference reconvened in February 1933, the French were proposing putting Germany on a 4-year probation period: if the Germans kept the peace during that time, then France would start disarming, but not before. The other powers went along with the French proposal; this allowed Hitler to complain that they had abandoned the principle of equal treatment agreed at Locarno and provided him with grounds for withdrawing from both the conference and the League. The result was that Hitler appeared to occupy the moral high ground while the British and French angrily blamed each other for the conference's collapse.

Financing rearmament

Rearming in the middle of a worldwide slump would require careful economic management. The budget for it was drawn up as early as April 1933. In effect rearmament was to be Germany's equivalent of Roosevelt's New Deal, which was launched at the same time. However, the New Deal sought to rejuvenate production of a whole range of goods for consumption at home and for export. Hitler's economic programme was entirely geared towards producing a stockpile of arms for future use. Producing the armaments would require heavy imports, especially of raw materials, such as oil, that Germany lacked; it also meant

Germany would be producing relatively little for export (because it could hardly start selling arms that under the Treaty of Versailles it was not supposed to possess). The result was a massive balance-of-trade deficit, with a corresponding drain on Germany's foreign currency reserves (used to buy imports) unless Schacht, as president of the Reichsbank, could come up with some way of producing extra credit. Large-scale borrowing was ruled out because the Treaty of Versailles imposed a low cap on the interest rates that Germany was allowed to pay; moreover, if Germany's deficit became too large it would alert the Allies to the probable cause.

Schacht's solution was the ingenious system of Mefo bills, issued by a front company called the *Metallurgische Forschungsgesellschaft* (Mefo, for short) set up to administer the scheme. Mefo bills could be exchanged for money and operated in effect as an alternative form of currency, enabling the government to pay arms manufacturers in Mefos without the payments appearing in the books. However, as they could not be used to pay for imports, they did little to address the Reichsbank's chronic shortage of foreign currency. Moreover, Schacht was unhappy with the idea of rebuilding an entire national economy on armaments: Mefo bills were no substitute for a manufacturing sector producing goods for export. By 1936 Hitler had concluded that Schacht's policies, however clever, could not produce the war economy he wanted. Schacht in turn was alarmed that Hitler was demanding far more of Germany's economic structure than it would bear. The result was the launch in 1936 of the Four-Year Plan, with Goering, not Schacht, in charge of it. This was an important example of orthodox policy making, in this case Schacht's approach to the stimulation of economic growth, coming into collision with the decidedly unorthodox Nazi demand for a nation geared for war. It was similar to the situation in which the German foreign ministry was increasingly finding itself.

The search for an ally

The main aim of any state's foreign policy is to safeguard its security. This can usually be done in one of three ways. First, the state can seek to make itself so powerful that no one will dare attack it; this is a highly risky strategy since it gambles on mistakes and weakness on the part of other powers. Second, a state can put its faith in a collective security system, whereby states act together to punish aggression. This was the basis of the League of Nations, but by the mid-1930s it was looking tarnished because of the League's failure to punish Japan for its invasion of Manchuria in 1931. The Locarno settlement offered a better model of collective security since it bound all the signatories into a set of mutually binding guarantees, which the others would step in to uphold. Although Locarno itself was dead in the water by 1933, the principle of collective great-power security was still alive: Mussolini pressed for a four-power security pact, which was signed in July 1933; however, since the French still insisted on strict adherence to the terms of Versailles, it had no real chance of success.

The third possibility was an old-style alliance. Alliances for war had been condemned by Wilson's Fourteen Points and by the Paris Peace Conference, but this was the form of diplomacy with which the German foreign ministry felt most at home. The ally Hitler really wanted was Britain, with whom von Neurath also sought to establish good relations. Brushing aside the Anglophobia of old imperialists such as von Blomberg and Schacht, Hitler engaged in a charm offensive through the 1930s, granting interviews to British journalists, receiving British visitors, including war veterans, cabinet members and the wartime prime minister, David Lloyd George. He made use of the British-born Prince Charles Edward, Duke of Saxe-Coburg and Gotha and the youngest grandson of Queen Victoria, whom Hitler appointed head of the German Red Cross and sent on official visits to Britain. However, Hitler's wooing of the British remained unrequited for the simple reason that, like the Kaiser before him, he could never understand how offensive the British found his style of government. Two events in 1934 made the prospect of a British alliance, never particularly strong, even more remote: the Night of the Long Knives and the attempted *putsch* in Austria.

The purge and the *putsch*, 1934

Fascist Italy might seem to modern eyes to have been the natural ally for Nazi Germany. Hitler had often spoken of his admiration for Mussolini's achievements in modernising Italy, and the two regimes appeared to have a lot in common, not least a deep hostility to communism and a penchant for murdering their opponents. However, Mussolini treasured his status as Europe's leading exponent of dictatorship and looked on Hitler as something of an upstart and an Austrian upstart at that. (Italian dislike for Austrians went back to the nineteenth century when the Austrians had ruled most of the Italian peninsula.) The Duce valued his links with Britain and France and was in no hurry to ditch them in favour of a close relationship with Germany. In June 1934 Hitler visited Venice, choosing unwisely to wear his civilian suit and raincoat, which made him look shabby next to Mussolini's resplendent uniform. Neither leader was particularly impressed with the other: the historian Piers Brendon points out that Hitler thought the fast trot-past of Italian troops ridiculous and that when he inspected an Italian warship he found the sailors' washing hanging where the flags should have been. Hitler had spoken in terms of a German–Italian partnership, but the Venice visit did not suggest that such an idea was a practicable proposition.

Hitler returned from Venice to face up to the threat to his position posed by Ernst Roehm and the radical elements within the SA. Roehm had alienated the other leading Nazis and the army leadership by pressing for a more socialist approach to domestic policy and proposing that the SA take over the running of the *Reichswehr*. Early on the morning of 30 June Roehm and his SA cronies were at a lakeside hotel in Bavaria when Hitler, Goebbels and an armed unit of SS rounded them up at gunpoint and drove them off to prison cells, where most of them were shot. Hitler then authorised a wider round-up of his political enemies and critics, including his own vice chancellor, Franz von Papen, who had made the mistake of criticising Hitler in public, ironically for not dealing more forcefully with the SA. The violence of this Night of the Long Knives, which the Nazis made no attempt to hide, had a profound effect abroad. Stalin and Mussolini were impressed, and the democracies taken aback, by this evidence of the regime's brutality. Hitler's justification for the purge was that Roehm had been plotting against him and that the government had to rein in its armed supporters when they were getting out of hand. Only weeks later, however, Hitler seemed to encourage just such a set of Nazi hotheads when they tried to seize power in Austria.

The Austria of the 1930s was not some perfect democracy in a picture-postcard setting; it was a deeply troubled and divided state. Stripped of its historic empire, it was a small republic, easily intimidated by its more powerful neighbours, France and Italy. The country was divided between conservative Austrians who clung to Austria's strong Catholic traditions, socialists and communists in the working-class districts of Vienna who wanted to establish a socialist republic, and the Nazis, most of them younger Austrians who were equally contemptuous of the old empire and of the republic and who wanted the country to be incorporated into Germany. The collapse of the Credit Anstalt bank in 1931 tipped Austria's already weak economy into meltdown, and in 1933 Chancellor Engelbert Dollfuss took matters into his own hands by closing down the Austrian parliament and setting up his own personal dictatorship. This prompted a workers' uprising in Vienna in February 1934, which was savagely put down, the troops aiming their artillery directly at the workers' flats. This was the context for the *putsch* attempt launched in July by elements within the Austrian SS, who had been specially trained for it at Dachau. The *putsch* was badly planned: the Austrian SA, angry about the SS's role in the Night of the Long Knives, refused to help, and the whole affair might have petered out quickly had not some SS men spotted Dollfuss and shot him. Mussolini rushed troops to the Brenner Pass, Italy's border with Austria, ready to invade at the first sign of military movement by the Germans. Hitler hurriedly back-pedalled and disowned the *putsch*, blaming it on undisciplined elements within the Austrian branch of the party. The Austrian minister of justice, Kurt von Schuschnigg, took over the government, running it in authoritarian style along traditional Catholic, rather than Nazi, lines.

The Austrian *putsch* was a setback for Hitler, undoing much of the work he had done since January 1933 to build a positive image for himself abroad. Either he had planned to take over Austria by force, in defiance of the Treaty of Versailles, or else he had no control over his own followers: either way his international standing was damaged. Alarmed, Mussolini gathered the British and French together in the Stresa Front coalition, specifically aimed at preventing a repetition of Germany's assault on the Austrian government. At this point, by any normal measurement, Hitler's foreign policy was an abject failure. He had pulled Germany out of the League of Nations but failed to gain a single ally, and he had driven the British, French and Italians to sink their differences in a united front specifically designed to resist him. Yet within a year he had reversed the situation and established Germany in a dominating position.

The rise of von Ribbentrop

Hitler's success in recovering from the Austrian debacle was due to a combination of skill and good fortune. To mend fences with the Austrians he released von Papen from prison and sent him to Vienna as ambassador, where the aristocratic former chancellor made a good impression. To help mend relations with Mussolini he renounced any German claims to the South Tyrol, a German-speaking area that, since being ceded to Italy in the 1919 settlement, had been ruthlessly Italianised. In January 1935 he was able to knock down another of the pillars of the Versailles settlement by engineering the plebiscite in the Saarland so that 90% of the population voted for reunification with Germany.

His greatest achievement of 1935, however, was the Anglo-German Naval Agreement. This was important not just in its own terms but because it marked the emergence onto the German foreign policy scene of Joachim von Ribbentrop. A former champagne salesman, von Ribbentrop had lived for a time in Canada and the United States. This set him apart from the other leading Nazis, most of whom had travelled little, and, combined with his shameless flattery and sycophancy, it marked von Ribbentrop in Hitler's eyes as an expert in foreign affairs. Von Ribbentrop's approach to foreign policy was consistently geared towards promoting his own career, usually by presenting Hitler with what he wanted regardless of the diplomatic consequences. He also developed a deep dislike for the British, which ran counter both to von Neurath's more positive attitude and to Hitler's desire for a British alliance. Von Ribbentrop's vanity won him few friends — most of the leading Nazis loathed him — but from 1935 Hitler began to use him virtually as an alternative foreign minister.

In March 1935 Hitler defiantly announced that Germany was rearming, and the same month he received a visit from the British foreign secretary, Sir John Simon, and the lord privy seal, Anthony Eden. The British were anxious to bring Germany back into the international community, ideally into the League. Hitler, who wanted an alliance with Britain but had no intention of rejoining the League, cannily played on Britain's long-standing support for equal treatment for Germany, stressing that equal treatment did not mean that Germany was claiming equality in armaments. The British had no grounds for resisting an agreement that would put the principle of equal treatment into practice. Von Neurath was sceptical about the chances of the British agreeing to Germany expanding its fleet even within limits and was therefore happy to let von Ribbentrop undertake the negotiating. However, von Neurath had not realised that the British were under strong pressure from their overseas dominions, which were concerned about the rising power of Japan, to reach a settlement with Germany so they could concentrate their fleet in the Far East. Under the terms of the Anglo-German Naval Agreement the British gave their consent to Germany's building up a fleet that would be 35% of the tonnage of the Royal Navy and include submarines. Hitler was delighted and von Ribbentrop returned to Berlin in triumph.

From Hitler's point of view, the political impact of the agreement was even more important. The French were furious with the British for signing a separate agreement with Germany in defiance of the terms of the Stresa Front; in their anger they turned to the Russians and signed a non-aggression pact with them in May 1935. Hitler was then able to use this revival of the pre-war Franco–Russian alliance to justify both Germany's rearmament programme and the naval agreement with Britain. Once again, as with the withdrawal from the League, Hitler was able to make his defiance of Versailles appear principled and the other powers look vindictive or confused.

Von Ribbentrop now lobbied Hitler for an agreement with Japan, which he dubbed the Anti-Comintern Pact. An anti-Bolshevik stand was always likely to play well in Hitler's eyes, but since Stalin had renounced the idea of world revolution and was in the process of having the leadership of the Comintern purged and shot, there was arguably little need for such a pact in the first place. The pact bound neither party to do anything, not even to share plans. Germany did not tell Japan in advance about its intention to attack the Soviet Union in

1941 and the Japanese did not tell the Germans about their plans to attack Pearl Harbor later the same year. The pact did, however, provoke a major split in the German government between those who favoured the Japanese, and therefore the pact, and those who favoured Japan's enemy, China. Both the foreign ministry and the army, who had established strong links with the Chinese leader, Chiang Kai-shek, opposed von Ribbentrop's proposal. Goering, too, was opposed to the pact at first, but came round because he wanted to get hold of Chinese raw materials for the Four-Year Plan. The pact was essentially an empty gesture of defiance against Stalin, who was not actually planning on attacking either signatory; however, it did undoubtedly help promote the career of its architect, Joachim von Ribbentrop, who was promptly despatched as ambassador to London, to get the British to join it.

Abyssinia

Mussolini's decision to invade Abyssinia was entirely an issue of national prestige, to eradicate the memory of Italy's 1896 defeat at the Abyssinians' hands at the Battle of Adowa. Abyssinia was a member of the League of Nations, which could not possibly ignore the invasion of one of its member states by another. From Hitler's point of view the crisis presented the useful prospect that it might separate Italy from the British and French, whose anger at Italian aggression in Abyssinia was coupled with general disgust with the behaviour of the Italian delegates, booing and heckling when the Abyssinian emperor, Haile Selassie, made his dignified address to the General Assembly of the League of Nations; all of which seemed to point to a definitive split between the western powers and Mussolini's regime. Hitler's only worry was that the three powers might patch up their differences and reach a deal. Ironically, this was exactly what the British and French foreign ministers, Sir Samuel Hoare and Pierre Laval, came close to doing with their plan to partition Abyssinia, leaving the majority of the country in Italian hands.

The Hoare–Laval Pact might well have been acceptable to Mussolini, but the idea of rewarding Italy for an act of naked aggression caused such a public outcry in Britain and France that the plan was never implemented. Hoare and Laval were forced from office and the British and French moved instead for a regime of sanctions, which angered the Italians without seriously impeding their war effort. The result might have been predicted: Mussolini withdrew from the League, as Japan and Germany had done before him. Encouraged by Count Ciano, Mussolini's pro-German son-in-law and foreign minister, the Duce turned for support to Germany. Worried that Hitler might send troops to help the Italians (who were having difficulties and could have done with the assistance), the British ambassador in Berlin, Sir Eric Phipps, tried to entice Hitler away from Mussolini with the possibility of an air pact with Britain and France along the lines of the Anglo-German Naval Agreement, but Hitler was not interested: he had already decided to issue the most dramatic challenge yet to the Versailles settlement by sending German troops into the Rhineland.

The remilitarisation of the Rhineland

It is often thought that the remilitarisation of the Rhineland was the start of the process of German aggression that would lead inexorably to war in 1939. Since Germany's military strength was still much less than France's, the Allies have often been blamed for not reacting forcibly to this act of open defiance. However, Hitler had carefully calculated the risk. His main concern was that the French might invade, and his commanders had instructions to pull back if they did. However, this could still have involved shooting and he knew, from the French occupation of the Ruhr in 1923, that the political repercussions of a shooting incident on German territory would almost certainly work to Germany's advantage. For precisely that reason the French were not prepared to move without a clear expression of support from the British who, as Hitler well knew, were not keen to provoke an international crisis, still less a war, to uphold a discredited treaty whose provisions were gradually being reversed. British action was even more unlikely, given that Mussolini had made it clear that Italy would not oppose the German move. With his characteristic eye for the moral high ground, Hitler followed up the remilitarisation with an offer to demilitarise the Rhineland again if the French would do the same on their side of the frontier. The French rejected the offer, as he knew they would, but it was difficult to deny the logic that underlay it.

The Spanish Civil War

After the Rhineland crisis it became more common to hear people talk in fearful but resigned terms of a war that was bound to come, not least because 1936 did indeed see the outbreak of a European war that quickly drew in people from all over the continent and beyond. The Spanish Civil War was sparked by the decision of General Francisco Franco to defy the elected government of Spain by leading a military invasion from his military base in Morocco. The Spanish government was the Popular Front, a radical left-wing coalition ranging from liberals to anarchists. Franco's supporters, known as Nationalists, rejected the Popular Front's politics, particularly its deep hostility to the Catholic Church. The conflict was therefore couched in ideological terms from the start, and the Popular Front, known in the war as the Republicans, appealed to like-minded people around the world for help. The British and French governments decided on a policy of strict neutrality and non-intervention, but they were up against the Soviet Union, which sent money and arms to the Republicans, and Italy, which sent troops to help Franco.

To the German foreign office it was clear that the British and French response was the correct one. Von Neurath was appalled at Hitler's decision to support Franco. Goering and his *Luftwaffe*, who would principally be involved in the operation, were delighted. German help to Franco was channelled through the Condor Legion, a bomber squadron led by General Hugo Sperrle and Colonel Wolfram von Richthofen, which won a fearsome reputation, especially after its notorious raid on the Basque town of Guernica in April 1937. The war has often been called a 'rehearsal' for the Second World War; it certainly foreshadowed some of the horrors that the rest of the continent would suffer a few years later. The Condor Legion was perfecting the dive-bombing techniques — swooping down on buildings, military installations or columns of refugees — that would be central to *blitzkrieg*. However, the war also set some worrying precedents, which were noted by the foreign ministry and particularly by the army. Hitler had confidently expected the war to be over quickly, but it dragged on until Madrid finally fell to Franco in March 1939. The Italian troops performed disappointingly and their opponents maintained an effective guerrilla campaign, both factors that would hinder the German war effort in the near future. Hitler was keen to win territory for the Reich through a quick military victory over his neighbours, but the experience of Spain suggested that even Germany's shock and awe tactics would not necessarily be enough to determine the course and outcome of every military campaign on which he might want to embark.

Questions

1 How much attention should historians pay to *Mein Kampf* if they want an explanation of Nazi foreign policy?
2 Do you agree that German foreign policy was the result of such random factors and individuals that there cannot be said to have been a policy at all?
3 What were the principal successes of German foreign policy in the period 1933–36?

The foreign policy of the great powers

How did Germany's foreign policy priorities relate to the foreign policies pursued by the other great powers? This chapter looks at the factors that, in the 1930s, determined the foreign policies of France, Great Britain, the Soviet Union, Italy and the United States.

France

France had to adjust to the role of victor. Not since Napoleon had the French crushed a major European power. France had by far the biggest army of any League member nation, but its military advantage would not last long: the Great War had devastated her young adult male population and hit the country's birth rate, and there would be a shortage of men reaching military age by the late 1930s. Even more worrying were the country's internal divisions. French politics swung between radical groups on the right and the left. In 1919 a right-wing coalition, the *Bloc National*, won a crushing victory in the elections; 5 years later it was the turn of the left-wing *Cartel des Gauches*. In 1920 the *Parti Communiste Français* was founded and affiliated itself to the Comintern in Moscow; by the 1930s it was opposed by a range of extreme right-wing groups, such as *Action Française*. Political conflict often spilled over into violence on the streets; by the late 1930s France seemed only one crisis away from civil war, the fate that befell Spain in 1936.

The delicate state of French internal politics was closely linked to foreign affairs and rearmament. The army had long been linked to the political right, so the French left tended to oppose rearmament. In 1936, however, the left-wing Popular Front coalition gained power under Léon Blum and immediately faced calls on the left for rearmament against Franco's Nationalists in Spain; now the right wing mobilised against this 'left-wing' rearmament. These mutual fears and suspicions effectively tied the hands of French governments, rendering rearmament a high-risk strategy that might bring political defeat or worse.

French alliances with central and eastern Europe

Despite the risks attendant upon rearmament, by 1930 France's foreign policy had committed the country to a range of alliances in eastern and central Europe, all of which carried the possibility of military deployment. The 1919 settlement had established a string of independent 'successor states' to the old Austro–Hungarian and Ottoman empires, all of them theoretically committed to democracy and the League of Nations, but in reality envious of each other's territory and fearful of attack, whether by a resurgent Germany, an expansionist Russia or, more likely, a vengeful Hungary. In 1920–21 Czechoslovakia, Romania and Yugoslavia signed a set of mutual-defence pacts that was nicknamed the Little Entente. France, in its new role as guarantor of European peace and security, signed a series of separate defence treaties with each of the Little Entente countries, including a full treaty of alliance and friendship with Czechoslovakia, plus a treaty of alliance with Poland. This policy made sense in the 1920s, when France was militarily strong and Germany weak; however, in the 1930s, it meant the French were committed to military action that, for fear of internal divisions, they hardly dared take.

France's difficult relationship with Britain

One solution to France's dilemma might have been a commitment to joint military action with Britain, but this possibility was scuppered by the disastrous 1923 occupation of the Ruhr. It is impossible to overestimate the humiliating impact this had on the French, especially as the right of states to take what action they deemed necessary if Germany reneged on its reparations payments was expressly written into the Treaty of Versailles. The French pointed the finger of blame partly at their own premier, Raymond Poincaré, but mainly at the 'perfidious English', who had been vocal in their criticism of the French. The crisis left the French with the resolution never again to take unilateral military action; this in turn meant that, from 1925 onwards, when the first French soldiers began withdrawing from the Ruhr, the initiative in European affairs increasingly lay with the British.

Such a close reliance on Britain was fraught with difficulties. Lloyd George had been deeply concerned that the French had turned the Paris conference into a vehicle for national revenge, and most British opinion saw the French occupation of the Ruhr in the same light, especially as the Germans had only been seeking a temporary suspension of reparations payments in the first place. Indeed, the British increasingly viewed French demands for general security as an excuse for domination of the continent. Ramsay MacDonald angrily declared in 1930: 'Security has become the most brazen-faced word in the language. She is a French strumpet.'

The onset of worldwide economic depression did nothing to soften France's hard-line attitude. The British were dismayed that the French insisted that Germany continue to pay reparations right up to 1932. Even worse was Paris's move in 1931 to destabilise the economic infrastructure of Austria. This was when, in an effort to deal with the effects of the economic slump, the Austrian government had announced plans to form a customs union with Weimar Germany. In France this evoked uneasy memories of the old *Zollverein* customs union formed in the 1830s, which had paved the way for the creation of a united Germany in 1871. The French response was to withdraw funds from the main Austrian bank, the Credit Anstalt, thus plunging the whole Austrian credit system and the economic infrastructure of Germany into chaos. Paris agreed to bale the Austrians out only if they abandoned the customs union plan and effectively handed over control of their economy to the French. France got its way, but the incident gave British ministers a profound mistrust of France's professed good intentions.

France's 'Maginot mentality'

By the early 1930s, in response to the falling birth rate and since it was in any case reluctant to take unilateral military initiatives, the French government had reduced the period of military conscription to just 1 year and begun building a massive line of fortifications, named the Maginot Line after the French minister of war, along the border with Germany. With its vast underground forts, network of tunnels, underground railway, long-range guns and anti-tank defences, the Maginot Line was undeniably impressive. However, the military reality was very different. The Maginot Line was far from complete by 1939: long stretches consisted of little more than trenches and barbed wire, and the line petered out at Luxembourg since the Belgians had objected to it being extended along their frontier. Most importantly, military thinking had moved on from the Great War. The development of tanks and aircraft had shifted the advantage away from defence and back to the attacker, as the Spanish Civil War vividly illustrated. Fortifications like Maginot might be a good way of surviving an attack, but they were no way of winning a war. The most serious defect of Maginot, however, was the development among the French of a 'Maginot mentality', an acceptance that conflict with Germany was inevitable and that there was little or nothing France could do to prevent it.

The French crisis of 1936

At this point France's political leadership imploded in a messy corruption scandal involving a shady character named Stavisky, who in January 1934 was found dead, officially by suicide though few believed it. The scandal brought down the government and brought the radical socialist Edouard Daladier to power. His appointment sparked off a right-wing protest meeting in Paris on 6 February 1934 at which shooting broke out and 15 people were killed. Daladier stepped down and a new right-wing Government of National Solidarity took over. By 1935 unemployment in France was three times its 1931 figure and industrial production was down to a third of what it had been in the 1920s. Agricultural prices slumped too, creating a crisis in the normally settled and conservative French countryside. France's highly politicised workforce mobilised, with significant numbers joining the Communist Party; large numbers joined the right-wing paramilitary groups in response. Finally, in 1936 France's foreign trade collapsed, the overvalued franc having made French exports too expensive to sell.

The effects of these internal problems on international affairs soon became apparent. In March 1936 Hitler sent troops into the demilitarised Rhineland, fully prepared to withdraw if the French moved in to stop him. They did not move, however, because the move came (as Hitler well knew) in the run-up to the French elections, and the government feared that precipitate military action might provoke a violent response within France. The government that emerged from those elections was a broad left-wing coalition known as the Popular Front, under the leadership of Léon Blum. Popular Fronts were set up in various countries in the 1930s — the Spanish one also won power in 1936 — and were widely seen in right-wing circles as a front for Communist Parties to gain power. The fact that Blum was Jewish only served to fuel the already strong anti-Semitism of many on the French right.

The election of the Popular Front plunged France into chaos. Workers at the Renault factory at Billancourt in Paris staged a sit-in to demand higher pay, paid holidays and a shorter working day, and almost a million workers came out on strike in sympathy, bringing the capital grinding to a halt. Blum conceded the workers' demands, which infuriated the right; then he cut government spending on social benefits, which infuriated the left. His refusal to intervene in the Spanish Civil War further angered the left; on the other hand, the right were angry that he turned a blind eye to the thousands of volunteers travelling through France to fight for the Spanish Republic. Right-wingers even had a catchphrase, 'Better Hitler than Blum.' In 1937 Blum finally gave in to the pressure and resigned; the caretaker government set up to replace him collapsed on 11 March 1938, the day that Hitler launched the *Anschluss* with Austria. With no government in office, no one had the authority to order the French army to move, even if anyone in Paris had wished to do so. By the time Daladier, Blum's former war minister, took office as prime minister in April, it was too late: Hitler controlled Austria.

France and appeasement

For France, therefore, appeasement was a matter of urgent political necessity. Rearmament or military action carried the risk of provoking civil war; moreover, Paris was increasingly aware of threats to France's overseas possessions from Italy and Japan. It therefore seemed sensible to do whatever was necessary to maintain peace with Germany, even if it meant appearing to give in to Hitler.

France's nightmare scenario was a crisis over Czechoslovakia. France was bound by treaty to help if Czechoslovakia were actually attacked by another country, so when Hitler started demanding land from the Czechs, the crucial issue for Paris was to resolve the issue without triggering the terms of the treaty. If the Germans were *allowed* in, France would be spared the necessity to go to war. The Czechs, on the other hand, were determined that the French should honour the terms of the treaty, especially as Prague had signed an agreement in 1935 with the Soviet Union by which the Russians promised to support the Czechs, but only if the French did too. This Soviet factor was bound to inflame the political divisions within France, so it made the French all the more determined to avoid war over Czechoslovakia if at all possible. The French government was in an impossible position. Daladier therefore had to leave the running of negotiations with Hitler to the British.

Great Britain

Before Neville Chamberlain came into office in 1937 prime ministers had generally left the formulation of foreign policy to the Foreign Office, only emerging onto the international scene at moments of particular crisis. As a result, the key figures in determining British foreign policy before 1937 were the foreign secretary, the civil servants within the Foreign Office and the diplomats in British embassies abroad.

The foreign secretary

Foreign secretaries up to 1937 had grown up in the tradition of diplomatic negotiation with men of a similar social background to themselves and were unprepared for Hitler's readiness to break with diplomatic convention. Sir John Simon, foreign secretary from 1931–35 under MacDonald, was wrong-footed by Hitler's withdrawal from the Disarmament Conference and the League of Nations in 1933. The 1935 Anglo-German Naval Agreement was Simon's pragmatic attempt to rescue something from that reverse. His successor, Sir Samuel Hoare, was similarly caught out when in 1935 he negotiated what he thought was a perfectly sensible resolution to the Abyssinian crisis with his French opposite number, Pierre Laval, dividing the country up in much the same way that Britain's pre-war *entente* agreements with France and Russia had divided up other colonial territories. The public outcry against the morality of the Hoare–Laval Pact was so strong that Baldwin was forced to sack Hoare and replace him with the younger Anthony Eden. Eden was prepared to take a tougher line with Mussolini, whom he saw as a political thug, but once Chamberlain was in power Eden found himself being bypassed by the prime minister's personal envoys, including Chamberlain's sister-in-law, who all negotiated with foreign governments and reported back directly to Downing Street. Eden felt undermined and resigned angrily in February 1938. He was replaced by Lord Halifax, a career diplomat and close ally of the prime minister.

Officials and diplomats

In practice, foreign policy is often formulated by officials rather than by politicians. Sir Robert Vansittart (later Lord Vansittart), who held the crucial post of permanent under-secretary at the Foreign Office from 1930 until January 1938, was a diplomat with a deep suspicion of German militarism, and he successfully pressed Baldwin's government to divert money into air defence. Chamberlain was less persuadable and replaced him in January 1938 with the more compliant Sir Alexander Cadogan. By the spring of 1938, therefore, Chamberlain had got his own supporters into all the key positions within the Foreign Office.

A similar change happened at the British embassy in Berlin, where in 1937 the anti-Nazi Sir Eric Phipps was replaced by Sir Neville Henderson, a career diplomat with a strong sense of the injustice of the Treaty of Versailles and a deep dislike of what he saw as French vindictiveness towards the Germans. Henderson was not actively pro-Nazi, but he valued highly his personal relations with the Nazi leadership and thought Czech sovereignty over the Sudetenland a poor excuse for risking another European war, a view shared by successive British ambassadors in Prague. Just as contemptuous of the Czechs was one of the most influential but curious of these loyal Chamberlainites, Sir Horace Wilson, a Treasury official with no diplomatic experience but whom, perhaps for that very reason, Chamberlain held in higher regard than he did the Foreign Office.

The highest-ranking of the Chamberlainites was Lord Halifax, who replaced Eden as foreign secretary in January 1938. Like Henderson, Halifax valued personal contacts with the Nazi leadership, although his 1937 hunting visit to

Goering got off to a disastrous start when he mistook Hitler for a footman and nearly gave him his coat to hold. Halifax's visit illustrated the extent of British miscalculation in dealing with the Nazis. Goering was genial and approachable but his influence on foreign policy was neither as strong nor as constant as the British supposed. Hitler shocked Halifax, a former viceroy of India, by suggesting over coffee and cakes that the British should put the Indian nationalist leader Gandhi and his followers against a wall and shoot them. Contrary to popular legend, Chamberlain was under no illusions about the true nature of Hitler's regime, but if he did not underestimate Hitler, he certainly overestimated his own ability to deal with him.

Churchill

One lonely parliamentary voice rang out in criticism of government policy: that of Winston Churchill. In his book *The Gathering Storm* Churchill presented himself as a solitary voice of wisdom ignored by a foolish government. In fact, Churchill had only himself to blame if he was ineffective. It was difficult for people to take his criticisms of government policy towards Germany seriously, especially since it was known that he had favoured reaching a settlement with Mussolini over Abyssinia. Churchill's criticisms gained bite when he started producing accurate statistical information about German aircraft manufacture, which he acquired through his friend Desmond Morton, head of the industrial intelligence centre of the Committee of Imperial Defence. Churchill was not in fact kept out of the loop by the government: he was taken onto the Committee of Imperial Defence, and his ally, Professor Frederick Lindemann, was taken onto the crucial Air Defence Research Committee. However, Lindemann proved so obstructive that he had to be sacked and Churchill undermined his own position by sticking obstinately to certain totally impracticable pet military proposals. It was the government's irritation with Churchill's impossible conduct that counted against him rather than any refusal on its part to face reality.

Neville Chamberlain

Chamberlain was so reviled in the postwar years that it is easy to overlook the adulation he received at the time. Even after more sympathetic recent treatments of him, Chamberlain still appears an incongruous figure with his hat and umbrella next to Hitler in his military uniform. Yet Chamberlain was far from naive. He followed the maxim laid down by the great nineteenth-century foreign secretary, George Canning, that it is foolish to take a strong diplomatic line without the military force with which to back it up. As chancellor of the exchequer Chamberlain had been responsible for financing Britain's rearmament programme, so he had a shrewd idea of its limitations. Britain's rearmament was geared towards aerial defence of the British mainland and naval defence of the empire. Sending a large military force across Europe, whether to help the Czechs, the Poles or, as Churchill himself discovered in 1940, the Finns, was quite beyond British capability and there was little point in pretending otherwise.

What was novel in Chamberlain's approach was his liking for meeting his opposite number in person. Hitler also liked doing this; he used such personal meetings to intimidate his opponents. This approach worked less well with Chamberlain, a man of enormous self-confidence who could talk just as toughly back to Hitler. However, it gave Chamberlain the idea, reinforced by the adulatory tone of much of the British news coverage, that he alone held the key to the future peace of Europe. He therefore kept foreign policy in his own hands, confident that both the cabinet and parliament would support him. Not until Hitler started upping his demands during the Sudetenland negotiations did the cabinet exert its authority and tell Chamberlain to take a tougher line; this was too late to be of any use to the Czechs, but it helped stiffen Chamberlain's nerve in dealing with German expansion the following year.

Defence of the empire

One of the biggest mistakes students can make in looking at this period is to spend too long poring over maps of *Europe*. Britain was the centre of a worldwide empire, and thinking in imperial terms came naturally to British statesmen. Hoare had been secretary of state for India; Halifax had been viceroy; Churchill had soldiered in India and Africa; and Chamberlain was the son of Joseph Chamberlain, the colonial secretary who had overseen British imperial expansion in the 1890s. By comparison, the British knew and cared much less for the affairs of central and eastern Europe. When Chamberlain described the Sudetenland problem as 'a quarrel in a far-away country between people of whom we know nothing', to many British people he was speaking no less than the truth.

The most obvious and direct threats to Britain's empire came not from Germany but from Italy and Japan. Mussolini's often-repeated demand for control of the Mediterranean — *mare nostrum* (our sea) as he called it — was a direct challenge to Britain, a non-Mediterranean power which nevertheless dominated the sea from its bases in Gibraltar, Malta, Cyprus and Egypt. The Japanese had shown themselves to be aggressive expansionists in their attacks in Manchuria (1931) and China (1937). When Chamberlain was risking war over the Sudetenland, the British-run international settlement in Shanghai was holding on by its fingertips as the Japanese overran the rest of the city. It seemed only a matter of time before Japan attacked European colonial possessions in Asia. However unpleasant Hitler might be, he represented much less of a direct threat to Britain and its interests than did the Italians and Japanese. The only real danger would come if he plunged Europe into war, but there seemed no reason why he should do that if his odd manner could be ignored and his demands addressed. Statesmen will not willingly choose war if they can attain the same goals without it, so Chamberlain's team thought appeasing Hitler the most obvious way to avoid a European war that would divert badly needed troops and resources from the Mediterranean and Pacific.

Defence policy

Ever since Cromwell's day the British had been deeply suspicious of peacetime armies. It was only after considerable debate that conscription had been introduced in 1916, the lowest point of the Great War, and it was dropped as soon as the war was over. There was no discernible taste in Britain for extending military service into peacetime, especially since the Great War was popularly supposed to have been fought to make wars unnecessary in the future. In 1919 the British government adopted a 10-year rule for military planning, which assumed that no major war was expected within the next 10 years. The League of Nations and the principle of collective security enjoyed widespread support in Britain. In 1933 students at Oxford passed a celebrated motion that they would in no circumstances fight for king and country, and in 1935 the League of Nations Union organised a Peace Ballot that elicited 10.5 million responses in favour of disarmament. Any rearmament programme that involved a large extension of the army was therefore bound to encounter significant opposition both within parliament and in the country.

The solution seemed to lie in air power. The Royal Air Force, created in 1918, had proved its worth in the 1920s in anti-insurgent operations in the mountainous regions of the British-mandated territory of Iraq; bombing raids had proved more effective in putting down the insurgents than military operations and at a fraction of the cost. It was widely assumed that any future war would consist of a series of vast, devastating air attacks that would utterly destroy major cities, an impression confirmed by newsreel footage from the wars in China and Spain. Accordingly, the priorities for British defence policy in the 1930s were expansion of the air force and navy, to protect the British homeland and Britain's overseas empire, coupled with a programme of civil defence against air attack. Hitler's remark to Sir John Simon in 1935 that Germany had attained parity with Britain in aircraft prompted Baldwin to replace the ineffectual air minister, Lord Londonderry, with the more dynamic Viscount Swinton. Swinton massively expanded the RAF from the 500 wooden biplanes it had in 1933 to three times that number of metal monoplanes by 1938, with a fourfold increase in personnel to go with it. Even this expansion of air power had to be carried out clandestinely, through 'shadow factories', which produced aircraft under cover of the car industry. Moreover, this rearmament programme did not provide for the sort of expansion of the army that would be needed if Britain were to play a major role on the European continent.

British foreign policy

The nature of Britain's rearmament, coupled with the tone of public opinion, therefore inclined Baldwin and Chamberlain to find a way of reaching an accommodation with Hitler's regime that would meet his legitimate claims without sparking a war. It made perfect sense to reach an agreement with Berlin in 1935 on German naval expansion, even though, as a bilateral agreement, it broke Britain's commitment to maintain a common diplomatic front with the French. Hitler hoped that the naval agreement would be followed by a wider-ranging association between the two countries. In 1936 he sent von Ribbentrop to London as ambassador with instructions to persuade the British to join the Anti-Comintern Pact, which Germany was negotiating with Japan. The idea of neutralising the Japanese threat to Britain's overseas possessions by joining a German–Japanese coalition, with the added advantage of doing the same to the Italian threat should Mussolini sign too, was not unattractive to Baldwin. However, given the obvious diplomatic difficulties such a step would cause with Paris, its negotiation would require careful diplomacy on the Germans' part. For this task von Ribbentrop was entirely unsuited. His boorish behaviour, even making the Hitler salute when he was received by King George VI, quickly made him universally loathed in London (the feeling was mutual). By the time Baldwin stepped down in 1937, it was clear that Britain would need some sort of negotiated settlement of territorial issues with Hitler but that any close association or alliance was out of the question.

Chamberlain's preferred solution was to stage a nineteenth-century-style congress, with himself playing the central role, brokering a general territorial settlement which would clear up the anomalies and injustices of the 1919 treaties. Eden and Vansittart were sceptical of Chamberlain's plans, which was why he began developing his own personal channels to the German leadership, including Halifax's 1937 hunting trip with Goering, and Lord Runciman's exploratory visit to Prague in July 1938, to sound out opinions on the status of the Sudetenland. By the time of the *Anschluss* in March 1938, Chamberlain's followers were in place and he was ready to take the lead in dealing with Hitler. That meant appreciating the merits of the German case without supporting the use of force. What the British did not understand until the very end was that Hitler *wanted* to take territory by force.

The Chamberlain–Halifax–Henderson approach to negotiating with Hitler lasted until after the Sudetenland negotiations of September 1938. The experience of dealing with Hitler face to face, and especially the abortive meeting at Bad Godesberg, to some extent dented Chamberlain's self-assurance. Cadogan was appalled that Chamberlain had not taken a tougher stand, and it was he who persuaded Halifax to threaten war if Hitler attempted to take the Sudetenland by force. Chamberlain still dreamt of playing the role of arbiter of Europe, which explains his elation at his invitation to the Munich conference, but it was soon clear that this was an idle dream. The famous 'piece of paper' that he persuaded Hitler to sign at Munich, containing a platitude about Britain and Germany hoping never to go to war again, was the last gasp of his dream of a British-brokered general peace. When public opinion hardened against the Munich agreement, especially after the *Kristallnacht* pogrom of November 1938 and the occupation of Czechoslovakia the following March, the changed mood was reflected in government. The cabinet refused to support any further appeasement, and by 1939 Halifax and Cadogan had lost confidence in Henderson, who himself described his mission to Germany as a failure.

The Soviet Union

It is natural for any student looking at the 1930s to assume that the Soviet Union must have been the unrelenting enemy of Nazi Germany and that it would have supported anyone wanting to take a strong line against Hitler. This was certainly the expectation of socialists and communists across the western world, who saw global politics as a titanic struggle between the forces of right and left, conducted in microcosm and in deadly reality in the Spanish Civil War. Stalin, however, did not share this view. For one thing, he was deeply suspicious of non-Russian communists, mainly because he could not control them; many communists who fled to the Soviet Union ended up in the gulag. Moreover, like many in Russia, he was acutely conscious that the real ideological opponents of communism were not the Fascists but the capitalist democracies. No one in the Communist Party of the Soviet Union (CPSU) forgot how the western allies had sent troops to intervene in the Russian Civil War in an attempt to strangle the Soviet regime at birth. Stalin's foreign minister, Maxim Litvinov, did believe in establishing good relations with the western powers, however, and worked well with his French opposite number, Louis Barthou, in the early 1930s, drawing up plans for a series of mutual-assistance pacts with the states of eastern Europe, but Barthou was assassinated in 1934 and was replaced by the more anti-Russian Pierre Laval. Litvinov even managed to secure American recognition for the Soviet Union, but it was no use: Stalin did not share his foreign minister's pro-western outlook. In May 1939 he replaced Litvinov with the more servile Molotov, who could be relied upon to frame foreign policy according to the leader's wishes.

By contrast with his suspicion of the democracies, Stalin had a healthy respect for Hitler. The two men were remodelling their countries in similar ways. Hitler's Four-Year Plan was clearly based on Stalin's Five-Year Plans, while Stalin was deeply impressed with Hitler's purge of opponents and rivals within the Nazi Party in the 1934 Night of the Long Knives. Counter-balancing Hitler's talk of *Lebensraum* in Russia was the obvious point that both Germany and the Soviet Union loathed Poland and the Baltic States, which had all been carved out of former German and Russian territory. For Stalin, this held out many possibilities for reaching a mutually advantageous settlement with the Germans, which would secure Russia's western border against attack, allowing him to concentrate his attention on the Japanese threat in the east, Japan's invasion of Manchuria having looked like the preliminary to an invasion of the Soviet Union. In 1939 Soviet and Japanese forces clashed at Nomanhan in Mongolia and, although the Japanese lost, Stalin could never discount the possibility that they might one day return in force. By 1938 he was busy purging the Red Army officer corps, and could not afford to undertake a war on two fronts; it therefore made good sense for him to reach a deal with the Germans along the lines that von Ribbentrop offered in August 1939.

Italy

Looking back at events in the 1930s it can be tempting to assume that Italy was bound to join itself to Nazi Germany simply because they were both militaristic right-wing dictatorships. This is a mistaken view because nationalistic concerns were every bit as important to Italian foreign policy as political ideology, possibly more so. The Italians had a long-standing grudge against the Germans, particularly the Austrians, that went back to the nineteenth century, and Mussolini, who was used to having other rulers emulate his style of government, had no intention of deferring to an upstart German copycat dictator, especially one of Austrian birth. The bungled Nazi attempt to seize power in Austria in 1934 outraged the Duce: Austria was within Italy's sphere of influence and the murdered chancellor, Engelbert Dollfuss, had been a useful figure who could be depended on to cooperate with Italian policy. There is a certain irony that it was Mussolini who, by sending troops to the Austrian border in 1934, took much firmer action against Hitler than Britain or France ever did before 1939.

Mussolini's aim was to have Italy accepted as a great power on the same footing as the established powers, Britain and France. This was why his instinct after the Austrian affair in 1934 was to draw closer to the democracies in the Stresa Front, a coalition expressly designed to keep Hitler's regime reined in. There was no reason why the Stresa Front should not have lasted: Britain and France both had a long tradition of supporting Italian nationalism, and public opinion in both countries was much more favourable towards Mussolini than towards Hitler. Even the invasion of Abyssinia need not have broken this British–French–Italian common front had the Hoare–Laval Pact not been rejected, which neither man anticipated it would be. The subsequent Anglo-French condemnation of Italy in the League of Nations angered Mussolini as much by its hypocrisy (because both countries had undertaken similar wars of colonial conquest) as by its ineffectiveness. The fact that League sanctions were so feeble suggested to Mussolini that neither country was as formidable as it liked to pretend; it therefore made sense in geopolitical terms for Mussolini to look afresh at the idea of an accommodation with Germany, first in the 1936 Rome–Berlin Axis and the following year by joining the Anti-Comintern Pact. Mussolini then turned his anger against the British and French, starting secret negotiations with Arab leaders aimed at undermining their position in North Africa and ejecting the British from Gibraltar.

Mussolini's newly assertive role came just at the point when the deficiencies in Italy's military prowess were being revealed to the world. His troops ran into difficulties in Abyssinia and had to resort to bombing raids with poison gas in order to take Addis Ababa, and the forces he sent to Spain proved so below par that Franco soon came to regard them as a liability. This revelation of Italian inadequacy had two main effects. On the one hand, it tied Italy more closely to Germany, whose airmen had distinguished themselves in Spain; on the other hand, it made Mussolini desperate to restrain Hitler from war until Italy should be ready for it, which he reckoned would not be before 1942 at the earliest. Mussolini maintained the pretence of power as long as possible, signing the tough-sounding Pact of Steel with Hitler in May 1939. However, Mussolini's alarm at discovering just how committed Hitler was to war lay behind his last-minute brokering of the Munich conference in September 1938 and his revelation to Hitler in 1939 that Italy would not be able to join Germany should war break out over Poland. This came as a blow to the Germans, who had taken the Italian's propaganda at its face value and thought they could rely on the support of a tough and determined ally. All sides took Italy seriously in the 1930s, and so should modern students.

The United States

The United States was preoccupied in the 1930s with the New Deal programme, designed to rebuild the American economy. Roosevelt was alarmed by Hitler but could do little more than send off ineffectual letters to Berlin because he knew there was no support in the United States for getting involved in European affairs. The Americans were suspicious of the League of Nations, angry with the British and French for reneging on their war debts and deeply opposed to any action that might involve sending American troops overseas. So strong was this opposition that in 1937 Congress passed legislation enforcing neutrality. Although Roosevelt sympathised with Britain's position, he found it difficult to get on with Chamberlain, who adopted a lofty and dismissive attitude towards the idea of American help. Moreover, the US ambassador in London, Joseph Kennedy, was deeply anti-British and painted a picture of Britain as doomed and best left to its fate, a point reinforced by the popular, fiery and deeply anti-British Irish–American 'radio priest', Father Charles Coughlin.

Other factors strengthened Roosevelt's case for intervention. The influential Jewish lobby helped to keep the anti-Nazi message alive, and Hitler's perceived snub to the black athlete Jesse Owens at the Berlin Olympics was not well received in the United States. King George VI and Queen Elizabeth made a successful state visit to Washington shortly after Edward VIII's abdication, and this helped to engender a more positive view of Britain among sceptical Americans. Nevertheless, it was not until 1941 that Roosevelt was able to get the Lend-Lease Act through Congress, which allowed Britain to obtain war supplies in America with payment deferred until after the war; even then, Congress made it clear that American aid to Britain was to be aid short of war. It took the Japanese attack on Pearl Harbor, later in 1941, to unite Americans behind the president's decision to abandon neutrality and declare war, and even then Congress would only back war with Japan. Hitler saved Roosevelt the trouble of winning Congress over by declaring war on the United States a few days after Pearl Harbor. He had little but contempt for the Americans and did not expect to find their armed forces too difficult to deal with. It proved to be one of his most serious miscalculations.

Questions

1 What were the principal reasons for the reluctance of Great Britain to oppose the foreign policy of Nazi Germany during this period?
2 'Appeasement was not weakness. It was a rational response to the realities of the 1930s.' How far do you agree with this assertion?
3 Examine the view that the most important reason for the success of Nazi foreign policy was the disunity of its potential enemies.

Nazi foreign policy, phase two: annexations, 1936–38

Starting with the military occupation of the Rhineland, Germany deliberately provoked a series of international crises between March 1936 and September 1939. Geared towards the expansion of its borders, these involved Austria, the Sudetenland, Bohemia–Moravia (i.e. the western areas of Czechoslovakia) and the Polish Corridor area of West Prussia. After the outbreak of war in September 1939 Germany annexed first a substantial area of western Poland and then the French border areas of Alsace and Lorraine, before finally over-running western Russia with a view to colonising it. Should historians view this programme of annexations as leading inexorably towards war, or is there a more nuanced way of understanding it?

The Rhineland, the Olympics and the Four-Year Plan: 1936

Hitler launched his policy of expansion in 1936, taking advantage of the divisions that had opened up between Britain, France and Italy over Abyssinia and the Spanish Civil War. Strictly, the remilitarisation of the Rhineland did not constitute expansion since it was within German territory, but, coming on top of the 1935 Saarland plebiscite, it constituted a powerful challenge to the Treaty of Versailles and a devastating riposte to the French, whose days of marching into German territory to impose their will were clearly at an end. Hitler pressed home his advantage by offering to sign a 25-year non-aggression pact and to pull his troops out of the Rhineland if the French would do the same on their side of the border, an offer he knew the French would refuse, thus making themselves look both vindictive and weak, as indeed it did. The need to guard its western frontier also meant that France could no longer think of acting as guarantor to the states of central Europe. This simple move within his own frontiers had therefore gained Hitler the same sort of diplomatic advantage as he might expect from expansion into a neighbouring state.

The Berlin Olympic Games, which Hitler's regime inherited from Weimar, offered the Nazis the chance to gain international acceptance. Various nations agonised over whether to boycott the games in protest at Nazi policies, but in the end only Republican Spain refused to attend, and many teams even made the Nazi salute when marching past Hitler's podium during the opening ceremony. The games undoubtedly helped to improve the regime's public image. Although anti-Jewish measures were suspended for the duration of the games, the racial agenda was never far from the surface; Hitler was not pleased at the success of black American athletes such as Jesse Owens, but it is not true that he stormed out of the stadium rather than present Owens's gold medal: after the first day he did not present medals to any athletes. Overall, the effect of the games was positive: opponents of the regime were never likely to be won over, but those without strong feelings about it were impressed by the efficiency of the organisation and the quality of the facilities.

The success of the games was all the more impressive because of the economic crisis Germany was facing by 1936. Germany's balance of trade was badly in the red as the nation's producers struggled to match the domestic demand for foreign imports. This was the consequence of trying to base economic recovery almost entirely on the arms industry. It was in an effort to resolve these contradictions that, in 1936, Hitler launched the Four-Year Plan, a programme to set up the economic infrastructure needed for full rearmament. Significantly, Hitler appointed Goering rather than Schacht as its director: the plan's priorities were to be military rather than economic. Such a broad restructuring of the German economy had its drawbacks because the plan was geared towards producing war materials at a rate so fast that it could not be sustained for long. By contrast, British rearmament was more geared towards creating the industrial infrastructure needed for a lengthy war. Whatever war Hitler finally decided to launch, therefore, he needed to both launch and win it quickly, and by 1942 at the latest.

It was in the same year, 1936, that von Ribbentrop's Anti-Comintern Pact between Germany and Japan was concluded. This was regarded by the German army and foreign office as a typical piece of von Ribbentrop self-promotion. Stalin had abandoned world revolution in favour of 'socialism in one country' and was putting the leadership of the Comintern on trial; there was little need for a pact to oppose such an obviously moribund organisation. Moreover, the terms of the pact did not bind the parties to take any sort of joint action or even to keep each other informed of their intentions, so it was difficult to see what it would do other than alarm Japan's enemy, China, with whom the German military had been carefully cultivating good relations. Goering, who loathed von Ribbentrop, came round to the idea of the pact only because he saw it as a means of getting hold of Chinese raw materials for the Four-Year Plan without having to pay for them.

Planning for war

The events of 1936 clearly showed that Germany had gained enormously in confidence and was beginning to flex its muscles, but did this mean that Hitler was intending to take Europe to war? The evidence that Hitler had a war in view is so strong that it can seem perverse to question it. Every one of these annexations, including the remilitarisation of the Rhineland, carried the risk of military conflict. German economic reconstruction from 1936 was explicitly based on a massive rearmament programme, including conscription. Above all, Nazi rhetoric, from *Mein Kampf* onwards, talked of war as a way of invigorating the German nation. War was implicit in all Hitler's talk of taking on Bolshevism or of gaining *Lebensraum* because no one believed the Russians were likely simply to move east to make way for the Germans. Professor Donald Cameron Watt wrote that Hitler 'willed, desired, lusted after war', while the German historian Joachim Fest thought that Hitler's sense of growing older made him all the more eager to launch a war before it was too late, a sort of grand political version of a mid-life crisis.

None of this means that Hitler intended the war he got: a general European war triggered by the issue of Polish sovereignty. Professors Richard Overy and Ian Kershaw are quite clear that this particular war was never Hitler's intention, while Tim Mason and Professor Gerald Weinberg see Hitler's desire for land in the east simply as his way of restoring a balance of power between Germany and the British and French empires. The war Hitler envisaged was a European crusade against the Soviet Union, to be launched in the early 1940s. The question for historians to ask might therefore be why things deviated so badly from the original plan.

Austria and the *Anschluss*, 1938

Austria's fate was sealed in September 1937 when Mussolini arrived in Berlin for a state visit. The Duce was acutely aware that his forces were not performing well in Spain and that his German hosts knew this. Moreover, Italy's breach with Britain and France was as wide as ever, so Mussolini had little choice but to ask for friendship with Germany — on Hitler's terms. Hitler had no wish to humiliate Mussolini, for whom he always retained profound respect and admiration, but he did want to remove Austria from Italy's sphere of influence to Germany's. Mussolini's acceptance of this meant admitting Italy's subordinate position, but it was clear to Mussolini that he had little choice. France's political divisions meant it was unlikely to take action to keep the Germans out of Austria; that only left Britain. But why should Britain want to halt a union (*Anschluss*) of Germany and Austria? It was hardly a radical idea. It made perfect ethnic sense and had been mooted since the nineteenth century. Hitler himself, Austrian by birth, seemed the embodiment of the close link between the two countries, and the Austrian Nazi Party was hardly less active or less ardent than the German Nazi Party. To Chamberlain, conceding German claims in central and eastern Europe, areas where no major British interests were involved, was an obvious way of beginning the process of mending relations with Berlin and diverting Hitler from making claims for the return of German colonies, which von Ribbentrop was enthusiastically encouraging him to do. On 19 November 1937, as part of his notorious hunting visit to Goering, Lord Halifax met Hitler and assured him that, as long as he obtained his ends without violence, Britain would not stand in his way if he wanted to expand in central Europe.

Armed with these assurances from London and Rome, early in the new year Hitler began to purge his advisory circle of conservative elements who urged dialogue in favour of Nazi Party loyalists who would do as he told them. Trumped-up sex scandals were used to force the army chiefs, von Blomberg and von Fritsch, to resign; in their place Hitler took over as supreme commander, with the subservient Field Marshal Keitel, nicknamed 'Lackey', as chief of the high command and General Jodl as head of the armed forces (both titles carried a lot less power than their names implied), and von Brauchitsch as army commander. In February 1938 Hitler finally replaced von Neurath with von Ribbentrop and Schacht with the less assertive (and less able) Walther Funk. Having removed the last of the restraining influences from his inner circle, Hitler was ready to move against independent Austria.

Even given that no one was likely to act to prevent the *Anschluss*, Hitler's path to his triumphal entry into Vienna was remarkably smooth. The Austrian government under Dr Kurt von Schuschnigg was failing to cope with a deepening economic crisis and there were widespread calls within Austria for unification with the more dynamic economy of Nazi Germany. Von Schuschnigg himself made Hitler's task easier: he was easily intimidated into accepting *Anschluss* by the Führer's ranting when the two men met at Berchtesgaden, but as soon as he got back to Vienna he renounced his pledge to Hitler and announced a plebiscite on Austrian independence. The wording of the question and the minimum voting age of 24 were clearly designed to favour the older generation within Austria who were most likely to give von Schuschnigg the No answer he wanted. He was, in short, using much the same electoral techniques Hitler himself had used in the Saarland, but without the military strength to back them up, should they be challenged. Hitler did challenge them, demanding that von Schuschnigg postpone the plebiscite by 2 weeks and substitute a differently slanted form of wording for the question, this time designed to encourage people to vote for an *Anschluss*. He also insisted that von Schuschnigg step down in favour of the Austrian Nazi leader Arthur Seyss-Inquart.

With the police powerless to stop the Austrian Nazis from causing mayhem on the streets, Goering sent a message to the Austrian president via Seyss-Inquart to say that if he did not sack von Schuschnigg Germany would invade. Von Schuschnigg bowed to the inevitable, cancelled the plebiscite and resigned, and the Austrian Nazi Party appealed officially to Berlin for help to restore order; Hitler got last-minute confirmation that Mussolini would not intervene and at 5.30 a.m. on 12 March 1938 German troops crossed the border. There was no resistance; this was a peaceful annexation, welcomed enthusiastically by the Austrian people, so there was no need for London or Paris to intervene. Everyone, with the exception of von Schuschnigg himself and a small core of older Austrian patriots, was satisfied with the outcome.

The Germans moved quickly to incorporate Austria into the Reich. Taking the opportunity to revisit his home area of Braunau and Linz, Hitler decided to annex the whole country and to absorb Ostmark, as the former country was henceforth to be known, into the Nazi economy. A huge military–industrial plant named after Hermann Goering was erected outside Linz and a new concentration camp was built above the nearby stone quarry at Mauthausen by prisoners sent specially from Dachau. Dachau itself was expanded to accommodate an influx of prisoners from Ostmark. The Austrians greeted Hitler's arrival in Vienna with scenes of hysterical excitement, and the Austrian Nazis promptly embarked on a programme of such savage public attacks on Jews that SS leader Reinhard Heydrich had to threaten them with dismissal if they did not restrain themselves. In the plebiscite held to offer retrospective approval of the *Anschluss*, the Catholic Church led the Yes campaign, which won 99.7% of the vote. This high level of support for the *Anschluss* encouraged Hitler to turn, as most governments in Europe expected he would, to the case of the Germans of the Sudetenland.

The Sudetenland, 1938

The Sudetenland had been part of the German-speaking territory of the old Austro–Hungarian Empire, and the annexation of Austria therefore strengthened the *prima facie* case for Germany's taking over the Sudetenland as well. As with Austria, Hitler could point to logic and history to support his case: it would be a reunification of the Sudetenland Germans with their former Austrian compatriots. Also, like Austria, the Sudetenland was going through a period of deep economic recession, and looked to union with Germany as a way out of it. International reception of the German case was greatly helped by Konrad Henlein, leader of the Sudeten Nazi Party, a man of considerable charm who came across well on the newsreels and made a particularly good impression on the British when he visited London early in 1938. Chamberlain, who was now working with the more appeasement-minded Halifax and Cadogan, reciprocated by sending Lord Runciman to Czechoslovakia in July to try to negotiate a settlement between the Sudetens and the Czech government. Runciman reported back that he had found Henlein easy-going and accommodating but that Beneš, the Czech president, had been pig-headed and obstinate. His recommendation was for some form of autonomy for the Sudeten Germans within Czechoslovakia, a proposal that struck Chamberlain as reasonable. With the dominions warning that they could see no case for war to break out over the fate of Czechoslovakia, and that they would not take part if it did, it seemed to Britain in summer 1938 that there was no reason why the Sudeten issue should not be settled as peacefully and satisfactorily as the Austrian one had been.

However, there were two major differences between the Austrian and the Czech cases. The first, which was obvious to all, was that, instead of involving the wholesale takeover of a German-speaking country, the Sudetenland question hinged on detaching part of a non-German-speaking country, and thus tearing up borders that had been drawn with so much trouble at the Paris conference only 20 years earlier. The second, which was not so obvious, was that the Czech issue was always conceived more in military terms than the *Anschluss* had been: Goering was keen to get hold of the Sudetenland's rich mineral resources for the Four-Year Plan, and the German high command had prepared a programme known as Case Green for a pre-emptive military strike against Czechoslovakia. This time, Hitler actually wanted to increase international tension and provoke conflict.

In the months after the *Anschluss*, therefore, Hitler advised Henlein to increase agitation in the Sudetenland, and he put pressure on Prague to accept the Karlsbad Programme of autonomy for the region coupled with a package of government economic aid. When, however, it became increasingly clear over the summer that he intended to follow this up with a demand that the region be incorporated into the Reich, his army commanders took fright, mindful of the impressive record of the Czech Legion during the Russian Civil War and alarmed at the strength of the Czech border defences, not to mention the risk that such an aggressive policy might provoke full-scale European war. Von Brauchitsch proved too spineless to speak out against Hitler but General Beck, chief of the general staff, resigned in protest at what he saw as a reckless drive for war with the western powers. At the same time, those conservatively minded officers who formed a covert opposition group now hoped that the British would take a tough line with Hitler and help them topple him.

Just as alarmed, however, was Goering, who blamed von Ribbentrop for this new and highly risky policy of confrontation over Czechoslovakia. Goering's office opened up secret channels of communication with the British to see if a peaceful solution might be possible. The British remained in touch with Goering, calculating correctly that he was a more pragmatic figure than Hitler and assuming wrongly that his was the major influence in German foreign policy. In fact, Goering, who wanted to keep the door open for negotiation with the British, was engaged in a power struggle for control of foreign policy with von Ribbentrop, who wanted to dismember the British empire. Hitler, who had not entirely given up hope of some sort of Anglo–German agreement, was more inclined to listen to Goering than to von Ribbentrop, but he was not prepared to compromise on his basic desire to take the Sudetenland by force.

On 30 August, acting on Runciman's report of his mission to Czechoslovakia, the British cabinet sent the Czech government what amounted to an ultimatum: agree to autonomy for the Sudetenland or face the consequences on your own. The Czechs, understandably, felt that they had no choice and on 5 September 1938 Beneš announced that the Sudetenland was henceforth a self-governing province of Czechoslovakia. Since this announcement effectively addressed all Henlein's complaints at a stroke, the Nazis had to come up with a fresh story to justify Hitler's clear wish to occupy the Sudetenland. So they started putting out tales of Czech brutality against Sudeten Germans. Suitably miserable-looking Sudeten Germans were then interviewed for the newsreels telling how they had only just escaped with their lives from the supposedly brutal Czech police. Hitler used these stories to stir up anti-Czech hysteria in his speech to the annual party congress on 12 September, demanding that Prague hand the Sudetenland over to Germany lock, stock and barrel, or face the military conse-quences. Beneš replied defiantly and it was into this combustible situation that Chamberlain came forward with a proposal that he fly to Berchtesgaden to meet Hitler face to face and negotiate a peaceful solution.

The Munich crisis

Chamberlain's dramatic decision to fly directly to meet Hitler face to face immediately placed the British prime minister at the centre of events. As we have seen, Chamberlain was acutely aware of the weakness of his position; on the other hand, he was no von Schuschnigg. When Hitler began the meeting at Berchtesgaden by denouncing the Czechs and demanding the Sudetenland be handed over to Germany forthwith, Chamberlain angrily retorted that if that was the best Hitler could come up with he might as well get back on the plane and fly home to London. Taken aback, Hitler started talking more reasonably, which was all the easier since Chamberlain was already convinced of the need for the Sudetenland either to govern itself or, more realistically, for it to be incorporated into Germany; the only point at issue was how and when this was to be achieved. The two men agreed on a process for deciding which areas should go to Germany, how this was to be done and what the timescale should be. It was this Berchtesgaden plan that Chamberlain agreed to sell to the French and Italians before presenting it to the Czechs effectively as a *fait accompli*. He would then report back to Hitler at a second meeting to be held a week later, at the spa town of Bad Godesberg. Chamberlain accordingly went to Paris for talks with Daladier, and the two governments then put joint diplomatic pressure on the Czechs to give up all land in the Sudetenland area where the population was at least 50% German, threatening to leave them to the Germans' mercy if they refused. Abandoned by their allies, the Czechs gave in and agreed to the Anglo–French plan on 21 September; Chamberlain boarded the plane back to Germany the following day.

The Bad Godesberg meeting went badly from the start and nearly started a European war. The two delegations were housed in hotels on opposite sides of the river, which gave the negotiations the flavour of confrontation between hostile camps. Chamberlain expected Hitler to be pleased with the concession he and Daladier had extracted from the Czechs; instead Hitler angrily denounced the unstable situation of the Sudetenland (which was in fact being carefully and deliberately created by the SA) and demanded that the Czechs hand the Sudetenland over to German control immediately; the precise frontiers could be settled at some later date. This demand, that Germany essentially help itself to Czech territory, was so unexpected and unacceptable that it seems to have caught Chamberlain off-guard. The most he could obtain from Hitler was an extension of the timescale for a German invasion of western Czechoslovakia until 1 October; for good measure, Hitler added an insistence that Hungarian and Polish claims to Czech territory should also be granted.

The Bad Godesberg meeting revealed just how risky Hitler's policy was. Chamberlain knew there was little chance of bringing his cabinet, let alone parliament, to support such a betrayal of the Czechs, going far beyond what had been agreed at Berchtesgaden. He flew back to London full of foreboding that war was only days away. Sure enough, the cabinet rejected the Bad Godesberg terms and Chamberlain sent Sir Horace Wilson to Berlin to tell Hitler so. Hitler, unused to the idea of a head of government being overruled by his subordinates, thought Chamberlain had acted in bad faith and shouted angrily that if England and France wanted to fight over Czechoslovakia, so be it: he did not care a *pfennig*. It was at this point, in late September 1938, that Britain and France began to mobilise their forces and organise anti-aircraft defences; on 27 September Chamberlain made his famous radio broadcast, saying how horrible and 'fantastic' (meaning 'impossible to believe', rather than 'wonderful') it was that Britain was preparing for war because of a quarrel in a far-away country between people of whom his audience knew nothing.

Despite Chamberlain's gloomy tone, Hitler was in greater danger in late September than he perhaps realised, as became clear when the Soviet archives were opened in the 1980s. Beneš was in touch with Moscow and had obtained a guarantee of Soviet support if France stood by the Czechs, which, in the new post-Godesberg atmosphere, seemed highly likely. With the German high command either too sycophantic or too scared to stand up to Hitler, it was left to one leading Nazi to try to save Germany from looming catastrophe. Hermann Goering used his personal contacts with the British, French and Italians to broker a deal whereby the Czechs would hand over only the German areas of the Sudetenland, with plebiscites to ascertain the wishes of the people in more marginal areas, all carried out to an ordered timetable. Goering managed to persuade Hitler to agree to talks and suggested that Mussolini might like to propose a four-power summit meeting to resolve the issue. Mussolini, who loved to think the fate of Europe revolved around him, issued the invitation, Chamberlain and Daladier accepted and the four leaders met in Munich on 29 September. There Mussolini presented a set of proposals that he passed off as his own but which were in fact the ones that Goering and the foreign office minister von Weizsäcker had drafted and got everyone to agree with. Leaving aside Teschen, which was given to Poland, and a strip of southern Slovakia, which went to Hungary, the Munich agreement thus formally agreed more or less exactly what Hitler and Chamberlain had agreed to at Berchtesgaden 2 weeks earlier; indeed in practice the Germans actually took over the areas Hitler had demanded at Bad Godesberg.

The Munich agreement undoubtedly saved Germany from war, but it is much harder to say exactly what form the war might have taken, and how closely

Britain and France might have cooperated with the Soviet Union in fighting it. Although the securing of peace was a bitter pill for Hitler to swallow, and he felt that Chamberlain had cheated him of a splendid victory parade, his generals were exultant since the outcome seemed to justify their opposition to his expansionist drive. German crowds, even in Hitler's beloved Munich, were jubilant at having been saved from war, and Chamberlain, not Hitler, was universally hailed as the man of the hour. It can be said that Munich made war in 1939 much more likely, not because Hitler was bound to demand more territory (there are good grounds for believing that this would have happened with or without Munich) but because it made him move away from Goering and towards von Ribbentrop and Himmler, men of limited military experience who favoured a showdown with Britain as soon as possible.

Questions

1 Examine the view that the most important aim of Nazi foreign policy in the period 1936–39 was the undoing of the Treaty of Versailles.
2 How justified was the view of Neville Chamberlain and his supporters that described them as 'guilty men'?
3 How far do the events of 1936–39 suggest that Hitler was not necessarily in control of events?

Nazi foreign policy, phase three: from *Kristallnacht* to war, 1938–39

Public reaction across Europe to the Munich agreement was one of profound relief, but this mood did not last long. As criticism of the agreement grew, Hitler's announcement after the conference that he had no further territorial demands in Europe gained wide circulation as a bad joke, as did the piece of paper, with its empty wish for peace, that Chamberlain waved so triumphantly at the aerodrome on his return from Munich. Two events in particular served to harden attitudes in the west towards Germany. The first was the sudden and violent assault on Germany's Jewish community that took place on the night of 9–10 November and became known as *Kristallnacht* (or *Reichskristallnacht* in full), the Reich's Night of Broken Glass. The second was the invasion and annexation in March 1939 of the post-Munich rump of Czechoslovakia.

Kristallnacht

With our knowledge of the subsequent history of the Holocaust, it is perhaps difficult to grasp the full significance of *Kristallnacht*. Life for German Jews had unquestionably been made steadily more difficult by 1938, and there were many cases of individuals being harassed or beaten in the street. However, there had been no organised programme of violence, and the great majority of the inmates of concentration camps were political prisoners. Anti-Semitism was a commonly encountered attitude throughout Europe (in Britain, for example, it was common to speak of going to 'the Jews' for a loan) and, although there was awareness that Nazi policy towards Jewish people was harsh, it was not necessarily believed to be violent or vindictive. *Kristallnacht* changed that perception.

The chain of events began in October 1938 with the expulsion from Germany of 12,000 Jews of Polish origin, many of whom had lived in Germany for years. The Polish government, itself no great lover of Jewish people, was unwilling to accept the full number, so that thousands of refugees found themselves stranded at the border. The teenage son of one such family, Herschel Grynszpan, was in hiding in Paris as an illegal refugee and decided to take personal revenge for what his family were going through. He bought a pistol, made his way to the German embassy, and asked to see the ambassador. Instead the third secretary, Ernst vom Rath, came out to see him and Grynszpan fired, wounding vom Rath fatally in the abdomen. Goebbels, who was out of favour with Hitler after the revelation that he had had an affair with a popular actress, seized on this opportunity to get back into Hitler's good books. He ensured saturation press coverage for the assassination and alerted SA units to organise a 'spontaneous' outbreak of righteous indignation against the whole German Jewish community. The result was an orgy of violence, most noticeably against Jewish-owned shops and property; some 200 synagogues were burnt down and the sheer number of broken shop windows gave rise to the *Kristallnacht* name. In addition, some 25,000 Jewish people were deported to concentration camps. Foreign observers were horrified, although some noted that ordinary Germans took no part in the attacks. The whole event was widely reported in the foreign press and provoked a storm of protest, especially in the United States. *Kristallnacht* revealed the brutality at the heart of the Nazi regime, making it much harder to uphold any sort of belief that Hitler could be dealt with according to normal rules of behaviour in any sphere, including foreign affairs.

The annexation of Bohemia–Moravia

Hitler's next move merely confirmed this impression. In March 1939 German troops occupied the remainder of post-Munich Czechoslovakia. This had been Hitler's intention all along, but it seems to have taken the rest of Europe by surprise. The Czech half of the country was incorporated into the Reich as the protectorate of Bohemia–Moravia, while a truncated Slovakia (the eastern province of Ruthenia was given to Hungary) was left as an 'independent' state, under German 'protection'. There were good historical reasons for this division of the country. Nineteenth-century German nationalists had always regarded the Bohemians (i.e. Czechs) as a Germanic people, whose proper place lay within the German Reich instead of in a separate state; this was why Hitler described his entry into Prague, uniting 'Czechia' with the Reich, as the happiest day of his life. The Slovaks, ethnically quite separate from the Czechs, had been vigorously demanding independence, encouraged by Goering, who hoped to use the Slovaks to get land concessions out of the Poles. In March 1939 the Czechs responded by overturning the Slovak government and imposing martial law. The Slovak leader, Father Jozef Tiso, under heavy pressure from Berlin, called on Germany to defend the independence of Slovakia; the actual declaration of independence was drawn up by von Ribbentrop and had to be translated into Slovak.

On 13 March the elderly Czech president, Dr Emil Hácha, travelled with his foreign minister to Berlin for urgent talks with Hitler. The atmosphere was deliberately intimidating: Hitler kept the Czechs waiting into the small hours and then subjected them to a chillingly calm explanation that if Hácha did not sign away his country's independence the Germans would launch a devastating attack on Czechoslovakia, including the bombing of Prague. The threat was reinforced by the presence of Field Marshal Keitel in full military uniform and by the fact that the two Czechs knew that German troops had already begun to cross the border. Hitler left them to mull things over, whereupon Goering and von Ribbentrop started shouting at them so much, thrusting the document under Hácha's nose and demanding that he sign, that the president, who had a heart condition, had a seizure and fainted. A doctor was called to revive him and as soon as Hácha was conscious a phone was put in his hand for him to speak to Prague. Still groggy, Hácha gave his cabinet instructions that the Germans were not to be resisted. Early on the morning of 14 March 1939 German troops crossed the border into Czechoslovakia and that country ceased to exist.

Although the invasion of Czechoslovakia looked in the newsreels like an assertion of German strength, it was also the result of German weakness. By early 1939 Germany's economy was teetering on the brink of collapse. The rearmament programme was proving unsustainable, even with all the economic resources of Austria and the Sudetenland. The national debt was soaring. There were serious labour shortages in the countryside, in the mines (which hit the railways and therefore the distribution of goods) and in the armaments industry itself. Germany desperately needed both foreign labour and foreign currency. In desperation, in January 1939 the directors of the Reichsbank, headed by Schacht as its president, called on Hitler to cut back on military spending or face financial ruin. Hitler simply ignored them and sacked Schacht, but even Hitler could not ignore economic reality for ever. Seizing Bohemia–Moravia gave him the bulk of Czechoslovakia's industrial plants, including the extensive Skoda armaments works. It meant the Four-Year Plan could keep going for another few months, long enough to launch a war with Poland. It also placed German troops on three sides of the Polish frontier.

The annexation of Bohemia–Moravia marked a significant shift in international relations and in German foreign policy. It reflected a decline in Goering's influence in favour of his rival, the fiercely anti-British von Ribbentrop. Hitler ordered an expansion of the German navy, to help with the programme of colonial expansion von Ribbentrop was urging on him, and welcomed Hungary into von Ribbentrop's beloved Anti-Comintern Pact. Ironically, the ease with which he took over Bohemia–Moravia convinced Hitler that the western powers would be unwilling to fight over Poland, whereas in fact the annexation finally killed off the policy of appeasement. Although kept in post at the Berlin embassy, Henderson was now completely discredited. Speaking in Birmingham on 17 March about the news from Prague, Chamberlain asked angrily: 'Is this the last attack upon a small state, or is it to be followed by others? Is this, in fact, a step in the direction of an attempt to dominate the world by force?' Since it was widely assumed that Hitler's next target would be the Polish Corridor, Chamberlain followed his speech by signing an agreement with Warsaw to guarantee Poland's independence. France also confirmed its military commitment to the Poles. In military terms these guarantees were a crazy idea, since there was virtually nothing Britain or France could do to help Poland directly, but they were a sign, which Hitler chose to ignore, that the western powers would fight if he attacked Poland. The only question was what role the Soviet Union would play in the conflict.

Memel

Before launching his attack on Poland, Hitler had one more territorial demand in Europe. The territory of Memel lay just over the northern border of East Prussia inside Lithuania. Its population was largely German but included a large Lithuanian minority. In line with his policy of incorporating all ethnic Germans into the Reich (even though by no means all Germans in the Baltic actually wanted to be in Germany), in March 1939 Hitler demanded that the Lithuanians hand the area over. Von Ribbentrop threatened military action if they refused. Mindful of what had happened to Czechoslovakia only days earlier, the Lithuanians gave in and ceded Memel to Germany. At the same time von Ribbentrop concluded an agreement with the Fascist government of Romania, which gave Germany access to the extensive Romanian oil fields. These moves were an important sign of the eastward direction in which Hitler was now turning his thoughts.

Poland

Poland suffered terribly in the Second World War, with its people singled out by the Nazis as slaves and possibly earmarked for extermination after the destruction of Europe's Jews, so that it is easy to overlook that, of all the nations to fall to the Nazis, the Poles had the least claim to be the innocent victims of unprovoked aggression. Poland had been dismembered by her neighbours in the eighteenth century, when most of the country was incorporated into tsarist Russia, which ruthlessly suppressed Polish nationalist risings. As a result, the Poles attended the 1919 Paris Peace Conference hungry for vengeance. They demanded huge swathes of German and Russian land, including the whole of Ukraine. In 1920 Poland provoked an aggressive war with the Soviet Union to expand her borders eastwards, and in 1938 took advantage of the Sudetenland crisis to occupy the Czech region of Teschen. Poland was ruled in the 1920s effectively as a military dictatorship under Marshal Pilsudski and, since the Poles were hardly less anti-communist, anti-Russian or anti-Semitic than the Nazis themselves, Poland might have enjoyed good relations with Germany had it not been for Nazi racial prejudices, which categorised them as Slav 'sub-humans'.

The borders drawn up in 1919 gave Poland a huge swathe of German territory known as the Polish Corridor, cutting East Prussia off from the rest of Germany. The port of Danzig was so indisputably German that there was no pretence that it should be considered Polish; it was administered by a League of Nations high commissioner, an Irish nationalist named Seán Lester. With encouragement from Berlin, the Nazi leader in Danzig, Albert Forster, demanded Lester agree to the city's incorporation into the Reich. When the League refused to support him, Lester resigned and was replaced by the equally hapless Swiss, Carl Burckhardt. With the Poles refusing to allow discussion of any change of status for Danzig, Forster started threatening German military action while also organising the intimidation of Polish customs officials. In January 1939 the German and Polish foreign ministers visited each others' capitals to discuss the growing crisis in Danzig and the possibility of Poland's granting Germany access across the Corridor; however, the Poles refused all concessions, and Hitler retaliated by making sure they were excluded from the final dismemberment of Czechoslovakia when he invaded in March.

The Führer was also making sure of his supporters in the coming war. He reassured his generals, whom he met in January 1939 to mend relations after the von Blomberg and von Fritsch affairs, that the western powers would not fight over Poland. Certainly the German people could not conceive that the British and French would fight over German Danzig when they had not fought over non-German Czechoslovakia. In May Germany signed the largely symbolic

Pact of Steel with Italy and also a series of strategically useful non-aggression pacts with Latvia, Estonia and Denmark. Hitler also read out in the Reichstag, with evident contempt, a personal appeal to him from President Roosevelt for a guarantee not to attack any of a long list of independent states. All this was merely preliminary, however, to Germany's important diplomatic business that summer: the negotiation of a diplomatic deal with Stalin.

The Nazi–Soviet Pact

The Nazi–Soviet Pact fitted much more neatly into the pattern of Soviet–German relations than many at the time thought, especially if viewed purely in terms of political ideology. Many Nazis were bewildered by what they thought was another of von Ribbentrop's over-complex and hare-brained schemes. Communists, both in the Soviet Union and outside, were equally astounded. Nevertheless, there was sound political logic in the move. Germany needed Soviet cooperation, or at least neutrality, in order to engulf Poland; the Russians had no cause to love the Poles and good reason to welcome a period of stability with Germany. Stalin and Hitler held each other in a certain grudging regard, and on the other hand Stalin was contemptuous of Britain and France, who had not thought to consult him before giving in to Hitler over the Sudeten crisis. In May 1939 Stalin sacked his Jewish and pro-western foreign minister, Litvinov, and replaced him with the more hardline Molotov, a sign that he was prepared to explore common ground with the Nazis. In August 1939 the British and French rather belatedly sent a joint military mission to Moscow to explore the possibility of joint military action. However, the mission travelled slowly as it went by sea, the two governments reckoning, probably rightly, that they would not get clearance to cross German airspace. Nor did it have the authority to conclude any sort of definite agreement, and this merely confirmed Stalin's already low opinion of the western powers. Hitler, by contrast, phoned the Kremlin directly and got Stalin to agree to receive von Ribbentrop in person. The pact was signed on 23 August.

The public terms of the pact constituted a non-aggression agreement, which was why most Germans greeted it so enthusiastically, thinking that it made a war, or at least a war on two fronts, much less likely. Its secret terms included a deal to carve up Poland and for the Soviet Union to take over the Baltic States; Stalin also handed over all those German communists and anti-fascists who had fled to the Soviet Union in the naive belief that it was a safe haven. Even after the pact, Hitler still hoped to detach Britain from Poland and to get a guarantee of British neutrality in the forthcoming war.

The last days of peace

In April 1939 Britain had agreed to a military alliance with Poland, and since the vast majority of the land Hitler had taken over had not in fact been part of pre-war Germany, it did not take a genius to realise that the Polish Corridor, which was entirely made up of former German territory, was likely to be his next target. The British move was warmly welcomed in Poland and it took the Germans by surprise. A coordinated Anglo–French offensive could wreck the carefully planned schedule for the Polish campaign, yet this move was so out of character for the British (who had studiously avoided such alliances ever since 1918 and were hardly in a position to lift a finger to help the Poles) that Hitler could scarcely bring himself to believe that London was serious. He met his generals on 22 August to reassure them that Britain and France could be discounted; he had seen their worth at Munich, he sneered. Nevertheless, the prospect of a war on two fronts, exactly the mistake Germany had made in 1914, did not appeal either to Hitler or to those around him. Right up to the last days of peace he worked to detach Britain from its alliance to Poland.

Von Ribbentrop now came forward with a proposal for a German guarantee to the British empire; in effect this meant that Britain could retain its empire if Germany allowed it to. The proposal, which the British were clearly going to reject, was entrusted to Henderson to take to London; the invasion of Poland was scheduled to start while he was still en route. However, the invasion was postponed when Mussolini wrote to Hitler to say Italy was not ready for war, and the British, who did indeed angrily reject von Ribbentrop's proposal, confirmed their alliance with Poland, as did the French. All this unwelcome news undermined von Ribbentrop's credibility and gave Goering the chance to make a more realistic approach to London, using as intermediary a Swedish business associate called Birger Dahlerus, who ascertained that the British were open to an arrangement but only as long as Germany refrained from using force. This news predictably threw Hitler into one of his tantrums. He then drew up a list of tough demands that Britain must agree to if war was to be avoided: an Anglo–German alliance, British help for Germany to take possession of Danzig and the Polish Corridor, the return of some of Germany's old colonial possessions and von Ribbentrop's idea of a German guarantee of the British empire. If Hitler was hoping the British would reject the terms outright, he was mistaken. Although London rejected the guarantee proposal, Halifax was prepared to discuss the return of German colonies and the status of Danzig, but not under the threat of force. Perhaps surprisingly, Hitler accepted the British terms, but he added that the Poles should now start nego-tiating seriously about Danzig and the Corridor, a point with which Halifax fully agreed.

A deal with London?

Was Hitler serious in this last-minute attempt to reach a peaceful settlement? He did not delay the mobilisation process, which would suggest he was not entirely serious. On the other hand, he did want to detach Britain from Poland if at all possible, especially as that would almost certainly cause France to keep out of war too. Goering took the possibility of a deal with London entirely seriously. Not only was he opening channels through Dahlerus, but he also used one of his Four-Year Plan staff, Helmuth Wohlthat, to open negotiations with Chamberlain's trusted crony, Sir Horace Wilson. From his vantage point at the head of the Four-Year Plan, Goering realised how dire Germany's economic situation was. The Reichsmark was overvalued, making German exports too expensive and flooding the market with imports, Germany's foreign currency reserves were plummeting, foreign investment was drying up, and the upshot was a serious fall in armaments production. The situation could not be solved simply by confiscating private property from Jews, but German Jews could have been forgiven for believing the government thought it could. Goering knew that, while a war with Poland might be over quickly, a war with Britain and France would be more likely to drag on and the Four-Year Plan simply could not cope. Even at this late stage, therefore, a deal with Britain was essential.

Hitler, however, had a much weaker understanding of the British than Goering and did not grasp how much the mood in Britain had changed since Munich. Having agreed to discuss Poland, Hitler tried the same trick of immediately raising the stakes as he had used the year before at Bad Godesberg. When he met Henderson on 29 August he demanded that Poland send a plenipotentiary (a representative with full powers to negotiate a deal on behalf of the Polish government) the very next day or the deal was off. Henderson protested at this ultimatum, but it was clear that Hitler was only interested in negotiating on his own terms. Hitler rejected an offer from Mussolini to mediate in the crisis and, when 30 August brought no Polish plenipotentiary to Berlin, von Ribbentrop summoned Henderson and read out Germany's final demands to Poland: the immediate cession of Danzig and the Corridor. Even Henderson could now see that this was not a regime with which he could do business.

On the night of 31 August men in Polish uniforms attacked a German radio station at Gleiwitz in Upper Silesia on the German side of the border with Poland, apparently killing a number of German personnel; the next day the German battleship *Schleswig-Holstein* responded by opening fire on a Polish munitions depot at Westerplatte. In reality the incident at Gleiwitz was staged: the 'Poles' were SS men and their victims were concentration-camp inmates, specially killed beforehand by lethal injection and now providing Germany with bogus grounds for abandoning diplomacy and embarking on war. The Germans followed up the Westerplatte attack with their full-scale invasion of Poland on 1 September. London instructed Henderson to tell Hitler to withdraw from Poland or face war. Hitler, unused to being on the receiving end of ultimatums, ignored the British demand. On the morning of 3 September, Henderson delivered the famous 'final note' to the German government, giving 11 a.m. as the deadline for notice of a German withdrawal. According to his interpreter, who read Henderson's note to him, Hitler looked drawn and shocked, hissing angrily at von Ribbentrop, who had finally got the war he had wanted, 'What now?'

The confusion of Nazi foreign-policy aims

Two themes had dominated Nazi foreign-policy thinking ever since the publication of *Mein Kampf* in 1924: first, a European crusade to crush the 'Jewish–Bolshevik' Soviet Union and, second, revenge on France for the humiliation of Versailles. The first theme clearly encapsulated Hitler's vision for the future and was the subject of all the loftier Nazi rhetoric. Alfred Rosenberg's *Myth of the Twentieth Century*, for example, was all about the falsehood of Marxism and why it should be uprooted from European soil. To ordinary Germans, however, moving into Wild West-style ranches in deepest Russia was the stuff of fantasy; what appealed to them was the idea of a quick military thrust to make the French eat dirt, followed by a triumphant parade down the Champs Elysées. No one seems to have asked whether these two aims, eastern and western, were actually compatible.

Both in *Mein Kampf* and in the Hossbach meeting Hitler spoke as if Germany could deal decisively with France, dust itself down and then turn to the proper business in hand, the destruction of Russia. This suggests that, despite the development of *blitzkrieg*, Nazi strategic planning had not advanced since the Schlieffen Plan, which had failed so comprehensively in 1914. Sure enough, the defeat of France in 1940 left Germany still at war with the global British empire, the very enemy Hitler had gone to such pains to avoid fighting. Moreover, the Nazi attitude towards the Soviet Union was itself contradictory. On the one hand, Hitler was convinced that the state of Russia was so poor that, as he put it in *Mein Kampf*, it was necessary only to kick the door in for the whole rotten edifice to come crashing down. This impression was reinforced by the effects of Stalin's purges on the Red Army's officer corps in the late 1930s and by the army's poor performance in the 1939 Winter War against the Finns. On the other hand, Hitler seemed only too aware of the size of the task: the Four-Year Plan was geared specifically (though not very successfully) towards creating the sort of military economy that would be needed for undertaking such a huge military enterprise. Hitler also had a vague notion that, eventually, from the commanding position of having conquered Europe and Asia, Greater Germany would have some sort of titanic clash with the United States for domination of the world; since he had a low opinion of the Americans, he had no doubt that Germany would come out on top. How serious this idea was is a matter of dispute.

It is often said that the British and French misread and underestimated Hitler, but Hitler's military planning shows him to be just as guilty of misunderstanding them. Having got away with the occupation of the Rhineland and the annexation of Austria, he assumed that he would be able to repeat the trick indefinitely. When he boasted that he had the measure of his opponents because he had seen them at Munich, he was forgetting just how close Germany had come to war over the Sudetenland. The idea that Britain and France would simply let Hitler take all the lands he wanted until he was ready to attack Russia showed he had learned nothing from the fate of the Hoare–Laval Pact. Moreover, President Roosevelt's much-mocked list of countries he wanted Hitler to promise not to attack was in fact a warning sign that even American neutrality might not hold if he continued to expand his borders in Europe. Hitler was acutely sensitive to how the German public received his foreign policy initiatives and was infuriated by the people of Munich cheering Chamberlain as peacemaker in 1938 and by the lack of public enthusiasm for the invasions of Czechoslovakia and Poland in 1939. Yet he never appreciated that democratic leaders would have to take even more note of public opinion in their own countries, or that it was not likely they would allow him to get away with annexing lands for ever. When, in 1939, Hitler declared himself baffled by Britain's declaration of war over the invasion of Poland when only the year before they had allowed him to walk into the Sudetenland, he showed a good command of logic but a poor understanding of politics.

Questions

1 To what extent did *Kristallnacht* make the outbreak of a European war more likely after November 1938?

2 To what extent does the Nazi–Soviet Pact of August 1939 demonstrate that ideology was never a very important part of Nazi foreign policy?

3 How far was the European war that broke out in September 1939 'a war for Danzig'?

Looking at documents and pictures

Documentary analysis

The Hossbach Memorandum

Memorandum

BERLIN, November 10, 1937.

Minutes of a Conference in the Reich Chancellery, Berlin, November 5, 1937, FROM 4:15 to 8:30 P.M.

Present:

The Führer and Chancellor,
Field Marshal von Blomberg, War Minister,
Colonel General Baron von Fritsch, Commander in Chief, Army,
Admiral Dr. h. c. Raeder, Commander in Chief, Navy,
Colonel General Goering, Commander in Chief, Luftwaffe,
Baron von Neurath, Foreign Minister,
Colonel Hossbach.

The Führer began by stating that the subject of the present conference was of such importance that its discussion would, in other countries, certainly be a matter for a full Cabinet meeting, but he, the Führer, had rejected the idea of making it a subject of discussion before the wider circle of the Reich Cabinet just because of the importance of the matter.

The Führer then continued:

The aim of German policy was to make secure and to preserve the racial community and to enlarge it. It was therefore a question of space.

The German racial community comprised over 85 million people and, by reason of their number and the narrow limits of habitable space in Europe, constituted a tightly packed racial core such as was not to be met in any other country and such as implied the right to a greater living space than in the case of other peoples...To arrest the decline of Germanism in Austria and Czechoslovakia was as little possible as to maintain the present level in Germany itself. Instead of increase, sterility was setting in, and in its train disorders of a social character must arise in course of time, since political and ideological ideas remain effective only so long as they furnish the basis for the realization of the essential vital demands of a people. Germany's future was therefore wholly conditional upon the solving of the need for space, and such a solution could be sought, of course, only for a foreseeable period of about one to three generations. …

German policy had to reckon with two hate-inspired antagonists, Britain and France, to whom a German colossus in the centre of Europe was a thorn in the flesh, and both countries were opposed to any further strengthening of Germany's position either in Europe or overseas; in support of this opposition they were able to count on the consensus of all their political parties.

Because of opposition from her Dominions, Britain could not cede any of her colonial possessions to us. After England's loss of prestige through the passing of Abyssinia into Italian possession, the return of East Africa was not to be expected. British concessions could at best be expressed in an offer to satisfy our colonial demands by the appropriation of colonies which were not British possessions e.g., [Portuguese] Angola. French concessions would probably take a similar line.

Serious discussion of the question of the return of colonies to us could not be entered upon except at a moment when Britain was in difficulties and the German Reich armed and strong. The Führer did not share the view that the [British] Empire was unshakable. Opposition to the Empire was to be found less in the countries conquered than among her competitors…The ratio of the population of the Empire to that of the motherland of 9:1 was a warning to us not, in our territorial expansion to allow the foundation constituted by the numerical strength of our own people to become too weak. …

For the improvement of our politico-military position our first objective, in the event of our being embroiled in war, must be to overthrow Czechoslovakia and Austria simultaneously in order to remove the threat to our flank in any possible operation against the West…Actually, the Führer believed that almost certainly Britain, and probably France as well, had already tacitly written off the Czechs and were reconciled to the fact that this question could be cleared up in due course by Germany… An attack by France without British support, and with the prospect of the offensive being brought to a standstill on our western fortifications, was hardly probable. Nor was a French march through Belgium and Holland without British support to be expected; nor would this course be contemplated by us in the event of a conflict with France, because it would certainly entail the hostility of Britain.

It would of course be necessary to maintain a strong defence on our western frontier during the prosecution of our attack on the Czechs and Austria. And in this connection it had to be remembered that the defence measures of the Czechs were growing year by year in strength and that the actual strength of the Austrian Army was also steadily increasing…The annexation of Czechoslovakia and Austria would mean an acquisition of foodstuffs for 5 to 6 million people, on the assumption that the compulsory emigration of 2 million people from Czechoslovakia and 1 million people from Austria was practicable. The incorporation of these two States with Germany meant a substantial advantage from the politico-military point of view, because it would mean shorter and better frontiers, the freeing of forces for other purposes, and the possibility of creating new units up to a level of about 12 divisions, that is, 1 new division per million inhabitants.

Commentary

The Hossbach Memorandum was an unofficial record of a 4-hour, unminuted meeting Hitler held on 5 November 1937 with von Neurath and the heads of the army, navy and *Luftwaffe*. Colonel Hossbach, Hitler's adjutant (a sort of military PA), took it upon himself to produce a detailed memorandum a few days later, summarising the discussion. An edited version of his memorandum was used at the Nuremberg Trial in 1946 to support the charge that the Germans had been planning to launch an aggressive war. Historians disagree, however, on its authenticity and significance.

The opening discussion of the *Lebensraum* idea is vague and entirely based on unsupported assertion; there is no attempt to define the 'space' that a people needs nor the concept of 'Germanism'. Hitler then reassures his military leaders that Britain and France are not as formidable as they look, again with little detailed evidence, and he offers some rather implausible speculation that the British might try to bargain with Germany by offering colonial possessions belonging to other people. He notes that the weakness of the British empire should serve as a warning to the Germans not to over-extend themselves, but to build a large and solid population base. He sees this as justification for his policy of expansion.

The military scenario Hitler describes is different from what actually happened. He envisages a simultaneous attack on Austria and Czechoslovakia, with no mention of detaching the Sudetenland. He is right in saying that the British had essentially written off the Czechs and that the French would be unlikely to take military action without British support, but both points were fairly obvious from even a cursory look at British and French foreign policy over the previous decade. The reference to forced emigration from Austria and Czechoslovakia shows that Hitler was accepting the need to use force to pursue his vision for eastern Europe and that war with France and Britain was probably inevitable; it is certainly important that he should have reassured his generals that the mighty British empire could be beaten.

However, the Hossbach Memorandum was clearly not the exact blueprint for war that the prosecutors at Nuremberg claimed it was. For one thing it has little detail; for another it records very little discussion by the others present, which sounds unlikely for a meeting that lasted 4 hours. In fact, it reads like one of those long, rambling monologues into the small hours to which Hitler used to subject his guests. It is true that Hitler approved Hossbach's draft, but he was always happy to sign pieces of paper without worrying too much about what they said. The memorandum shows that Hitler was anticipating major military action within a year or so. Beyond that, it is no more a guide to Hitler's intentions than Chamberlain's famous piece of paper.

Picture analysis

Source 1

AKG Images

This postcard shows a strong, healthy Austrian (the clue lies in the *lederhosen* — leather shorts popular in Austria and southern Germany) raising a keystone labelled *Anschluss* to complete the bridge between Austria, on the left, and Germany. The Austrians are shown clamouring to cross the bridge to join their welcoming German compatriots, symbolised by a flag-bearing character in the style of nineteenth-century nationalist figures. At first sight this image might seem to date from 1938, when Hitler actually did take over Austria, but in fact it was produced in 1921. That is why the figure representing Germany carries the black, red and gold flag of the Weimar Republic rather than either the black, white and red tricolour or the swastika flag adopted by the Nazi regime. The postcard was produced to persuade Austrians to vote for union with Germany and is therefore evidence of support for *Anschluss* long predating Hitler's rise to power. The postcard is a reminder that, for German nationalists, union between the two great German nations was not just desirable but essential. No bridge can survive without its keystone, nor, according to the artist, can either Germany or Austria survive without *Anschluss*.

Source 2

WHAT, NO CHAIR FOR ME ?

This cartoon by David Low appeared in the London *Evening Standard* on 30 September 1938, as the Munich conference convened. Low produced some of the most enduring and insightful cartoon commentaries on the international situation as it developed in the 1930s. At a time when much official opinion supported Chamberlain, Low remained resolutely critical of appeasement and scathing about Hitler, and he featured on a list of prominent figures in British public life that the Germans intended to round up when they overran Britain. In this cartoon, Low highlights one of the gravest weaknesses of the appeasers' policy: the exclusion from their negotiations of the Soviet Union. The four figures sit around a globe, a map of Czechoslovakia on the wall behind them, and, with no table, the conference looks tawdry and absurd. The self-satisfied air of the two dictators, their arms crossed, and Hitler having stowed the four-power pact in his cap, contrasts with the weak image of Chamberlain and Daladier, sitting with their hands between their knees like naughty schoolboys. Chamberlain and Daladier are the only ones to look round guiltily at Stalin's entrance; Hitler and Mussolini take no notice. Low is suggesting that the British and French should have invited the Russians and implying that they will be the ones to suffer from the consequences. The cartoon works because the idea is so simple and easily grasped; its very simplicity underlines the foolishness of the British and French in not recognising the need for Soviet support in the first place. Working with the Soviet Union was not going to be easy, and Chamberlain's central role in the crisis had perhaps enabled many in Britain to put the Russians out of their minds, but Low is here reminding them of political realities. The irony is that Hitler was more aware of Low's point than Chamberlain was; the result was the Nazi-Soviet Pact of the following year. Low came up with a suitably sardonic comment on that, too.

Chapter 1

Bibliography

The foreign policy of Nazi Germany is covered extensively in the standard accounts of the period. Some more detailed treatments that are worth looking at include the books listed below.

Klaus Hildebrand, *German Foreign Policy from Bismarck to Adenauer: The Limits of Statecraft*, Unwin Hyman, 1989

Hildebrand knocks firmly on the head the idea that there was anything 'weak' about Hitler's dictatorship:

> The attempt has been made, from a social imperialist perspective, to suggest that Hitler pursued his foreign policy in order to overcome internal crises; the foreign policy of the Führer is thus seen predominantly as a part of Nazi attempts to legitimize and consolidate power. This 'functionalist' view of Hitler's political objectives has led Hans Mommsen to reach a conclusion that I regard as wholly erroneous, in which Hitler is described as 'in many ways' 'a weak dictator'… So long as there are no reliable sources for the 'revisionist' thesis, we can continue to accept the assessment of Hitler's foreign policy objectives made by Norman Rich: 'These were all the policies and decisions of Hitler'. The American historian is emphatic: 'The point cannot be stressed too strongly: Hitler was master in the Third Reich.'

Gerhard L. Weinberg, *The Foreign Policy of Hitler's Germany: Diplomatic Revolution in Europe, 1933-36*, University of Chicago, 1970

We obviously need to consider Hitler's own understanding of foreign policy, and here Gerhard Weinberg outlines the situation with arresting candour:

> When Adolf Hitler became chancellor of Germany at the age of forty-three in 1933, he had held no previous position of authority in government. He had neither read intensively nor travelled extensively. He knew no foreign language. Yet he had a clearly formulated set of ideas on major issues of foreign policy. It is essential for an understanding of world history since 1933 that these ideas be examined in some detail, for a great part of the impact of Hitler on Germany — and of Germany on the world — lies precisely in the fact that by exertion of his will and the response it elicited inside Germany, Hitler was able to impress his ideas on events rather than allow events and realities to reshape his ideas.

Paul W. Doerr, *British Foreign Policy, 1919-1939: 'Hope for the Best, Prepare for the Worst'*, **Manchester University Press, 1998**

A grasp of British policy is also necessary. Paul W. Doerr gives a vivid description of the calibre of people staffing the British Foreign Office in the 1930s:

> Hope Vere, a melancholy dyspeptic little man, had distinguished himself on his first day in the ciphering room by sitting alone for about half an hour before suddenly announcing in his high squeaky voice: 'This telegram is marked Very Urgent and is totally indecipherable.'

Winston S. Churchill, *The Second World War, Vol. I, The Gathering Storm* (1948)

There is also Churchill's influential but selective memoir:

> It is baffling to reflect that what men call honour does not correspond always to Christian ethics...Here however the moment came when honour pointed the path of duty, and when also the right judgment of the facts at that time would have reinforced its dictates.

> For the French Government to leave her faithful ally Czechoslovakia to her fate was a melancholy lapse from which flowed terrible consequences. Not only wise and fair policy, but chivalry, honour, and sympathy for a small threatened people made an overwhelming concentration. Great Britain, who would certainly have fought if bound by treaty obligations, was nevertheless now deeply involved, and it must be recorded with regret that the British Government not only acquiesced but encouraged the French Government in a fatal course.

A. J. P. Taylor, *The Origins of the Second World War* (1961)

A. J. P. Taylor's analysis remains of central importance. This passage shows how his written style could read like an address to a party rally:

> The settlement at Munich was a triumph for British policy, which had worked precisely to this end; not a triumph for Hitler, who had started with no such clear intention. Nor was it a triumph for selfish or cynical British statesmen, indifferent to the fate of far-off peoples or calculating that Hitler might be launched into war against Soviet Russia. It was a triumph for all that was best and most enlightened in British life; a triumph for those who had preached equal justice between peoples; a triumph for those who had courageously denounced the harshness and short-sightedness of Versailles.

Piers Brendon, *The Dark Valley: A Panorama of the 1930s*, Johnathan Cape, 2000

Everyone should read Piers Brendon's account of the period, if only to savour his mischievous prose style:

> Actually [Lord] Halifax had no idea of how to cope with the Third Reich — he was like a eunuch in a brothel.

Glossary

Abyssinia

Modern-day Ethiopia. An ancient Christian kingdom ruled by the Emperor Haile Selassie, and a member of the League of Nations, it had fought off an Italian invasion in 1896 but was defeated when Mussolini launched a second invasion in 1935. In 1940 the Italians were driven out by the British, who restored Haile Selassie to the throne.

Anglo-German Naval Agreement, 1935

The first result of Hitler's search for an alliance with Britain. The agreement allowed Germany to build up a fleet 35% the size of Britain's in terms of tonnage.

Anschluss

The German word for 'union', usually applied to a union between Germany and Austria. Historically, Austria had played a leading role in Germany. The separation of the two countries dated only from the unification of Germany by Bismarck in 1871.

Anti-Comintern Pact, 1936

An anti-Communist agreement between Germany and Japan, brokered by von Ribbentrop. Italy, too, signed in 1937, followed by other countries in 1941. Although hostile to the Soviet Union, it was not a formal military alliance.

Baltic States

Estonia, Latvia and Lithuania. Although culturally Germanic, they were absorbed by Russia in the eighteenth and nineteenth centuries. They were taken from Russia under the Treaty of Brest-Litovsk and established as independent states by the Paris Peace Conference. Under the terms of the Nazi–Soviet Pact, they were allocated to the Soviet Union, which invaded and annexed them in 1940. Their peoples therefore generally welcomed the German invasion of the Soviet Union the following year.

Berchtesgaden

Town in the Bavarian Alps, where Hitler had a mountaintop home with magnificent views to which he liked to invite visitors. It was the scene of his first meeting with Neville Chamberlain during the Sudetenland crisis of September 1938.

Berlin, Treaty of

Agreement of 1926 between Germany and Russia confirming the terms of the Treaty of Rapallo and guaranteeing peace between the two countries for 5 years.

Blitzkrieg

German for 'lightning war'. A military strategy that involved co-ordinated attacks by tanks and dive-bombing aircraft, to destroy key military and logistical installations, including the opposing air force, terrorise civilians and spread so much panic and confusion that the enemy's forces would be unable to deploy effectively. It was designed to achieve complete victory speedily, enabling German leaders to incorporate short, decisive wars into their foreign policy.

Bohemia–Moravia

The two Czech-speaking regions of Czechoslovakia. German nationalists regarded them as ethnically German and they were annexed to Germany in March 1939.

Brest-Litovsk, Treaty of

Peace agreement signed between Wilhelmine Germany and Bolshevik Russia on 3 March 1918. Russia gave up a huge area of land in the west, including Poland, Ukraine and the Baltic States. By signing a separate peace with the Germans, the Russians were in breach of their alliance with the British and French and were therefore excluded from the Paris Peace Conference.

Case Green

The German plan for the military invasion of Czechoslovakia. Because the Munich agreement handed the Sudetenland to Germany without the need for war, the plan was never fully put into practice, but it did form the basis for the German takeover of Bohemia–Moravia in March 1939.

Catholic Centre Party

Also 'Centre Party'. German political party originally set up to defend the Catholic Church in Germany against attack by the state under Bismarck. It dissolved itself by order of the Pope under the terms of the Concordat signed between the Nazi government and the Vatican in 1933.

Comintern

Short for Communist International. An international association of communist parties under Russian leadership, which worked to foment worldwide communist revolution. Much feared by other governments, it prompted the formation of the Anti-Comintern Pact, but, in fact, Stalin's decision to concentrate on building socialism in the Soviet Union robbed the Comintern of any effective power.

Concordat

Latin for 'it is agreed'. The name used for any diplomatic agreement with the Holy See. An important Concordat was signed with Fascist Italy in 1922, which established the Vatican City as an independent state in return for papal support for the regime, and another was signed with Nazi Germany in 1933, which closed down the Catholic Centre Party and stifled Catholic opposition to Hitler's regime.

Condor Legion

The German air squadron sent to support Franco during the Spanish Civil War. It used the war to perfect the technique of close dive-bombing of civilian targets, most notoriously in an attack on the Basque market town of Guernica on 26 April 1937.

Credit Anstalt

The major Austrian bank between the wars. It provided the credit underpinning much of the German and Austrian economies until it collapsed in 1931, precipitating an economic crisis. Much of the blame for its collapse was laid at the door of the French government.

Czech Legion

A military unit set up by Czech soldiers stranded in Russia at the end of the First World War. It gained a formidable reputation during the Russian Civil War, which made German generals nervous about Hitler's plan to attack Czechoslovakia in 1938.

Czechoslovakia

A state, constituting the modern Czech Republic and Slovakia, created by the Paris Peace Conference out of a number of provinces of the old Habsburg Empire. Its main parts were Bohemia, Moravia and Slovakia, with part of Ruthenia. In order to provide the state with a defensible frontier, the Conference also gave it the German-speaking border region, Sudetenland.

Danzig

A German Baltic seaport, now the Polish city of Gdansk. The Paris Peace Conference intended Poland to have use of the city, but because its population was entirely German it was made a free city under the supervision of the League of Nations.

Dawes Plan

An international agreement brokered in 1924 by the American financier Charles Dawes to render the schedule of German reparations more manageable, with a regular schedule of payments and a ban on military action to enforce payment.

Disarmament Conference

An international conference set up by the League of Nations in 1932 to reach a general settlement on global arms reduction. It was rendered irrelevant when Germany withdrew from it in 1933.

Duce

Italian for 'leader', the political title taken by Mussolini, who considered it more dynamic than his official title of Prime Minister. Italy's head of state remained King Victor Emmanuel III.

Four-Year Plan

A centralised, coordinated plan of industrial development launched in Germany in 1936 to provide the economic basis for war. It was overseen by Goering rather than by an economic expert and failed to provide the economic infrastructure required for a long war.

Franco-Prussian War (1870–71)

War between the German states (led by Prussia) and France, which resulted in a catastrophic French defeat and the declaration of a united Germany. The German victory, overseen by Bismarck, provided the basis for German–French enmity in both the First and the Second World Wars.

Freikorps

Groups of former soldiers set up in Germany after the First World War to defend the country against what they saw as communist subversion. The name came from bands of nationalist volunteers who had fought against Napoleon in 1812–13.

Führer

German for 'leader', the political title taken by Hitler after Hindenburg's death in 1934. It combined the offices of president and chancellor into that of a single head of state.

General staff

The organising body of the German army. It oversaw all military planning, particularly the logistical requirements of military campaigns, and was widely regarded as the key to German military success in both world wars.

Hoare–Laval Pact

Anglo–French agreement of December 1935 to resolve the crisis created by the Italian invasion of Abyssinia. The British and French foreign ministers, Sir Samuel Hoare and Pierre Laval, proposed partitioning Abyssinia, leaving most of it in Italian hands. Both men were surprised by the furore their plan provoked and were forced to resign.

Glossary

Hossbach Memorandum

An unofficial account drawn up by Hitler's adjutant, Colonel Hossbach, of a meeting held in 1937 between Hitler and his military and diplomatic chiefs. The memorandum appeared to provide evidence that Hitler was planning to wage aggressive war against his European neighbours.

Irredentist

A term derived from the Italian phrase *Italia irredenta* ('Italy unredeemed') to denote a state's claim to all the lands inhabited, either now or in the past, by its ethnic group.

Isolationism

A tendency in American foreign policy in the first half of the twentieth century to draw away from involvement in European affairs.

Karlsbad Programme

A proposal agreed in 1938 between the Germans of the Sudetenland and the government of Czechoslovakia to allow self-government to the Sudeten Germans.

Kristallnacht

In English, 'night of broken glass', also *Reichskristallnacht*. A series of violent attacks on Jews and Jewish property in Germany organised by Goebbels in November 1938 in response to the assassination of a German diplomat in Paris by a young Polish–German Jew. The violence alienated foreign opinion that had supported the policy of appeasement.

League of Nations

International governmental body set up at President Wilson's insistence under the terms of the 1919 Paris Peace Settlement. Its capacity to impose peaceful settlements of international disputes was totally compromised by the non-adherence of the United States and the exclusion of Germany and the Soviet Union.

Lebensraum

Literally 'living space', the notion put forward by Hitler in *Mein Kampf* that the German nation needed more space in order to fulfil its destiny. *Lebensraum* was generally thought to lie in Russia and elsewhere in eastern Europe; the intention was that the resident population should either serve the new German settlers or be eliminated.

Lend-Lease Act

US Act of Congress passed in March 1941 whereby war materials were lent or leased to Britain and its allies, with payment deferred until after the war. It was a major departure from the US's policy of neutrality.

Little Entente
: A set of mutual defence pacts signed in 1920–21 between Yugoslavia, Romania and Czechoslovakia.

Locarno, Treaties of
: A series of international agreements signed at Locarno in Switzerland on 1 December 1925 between Britain, France, Germany and Italy to settle territorial disputes resulting from the Paris Peace Settlement and the Treaty of Versailles.

Mefo bills
: Credit notes devised by Hjalmar Schacht and ostensibly issued by a company called Metallurgische Forschung ('Mefo' for short), but in fact issued by the German government as a means of financing German rearmament.

Mein Kampf
: 'My Struggle', a book written by Hitler while in prison after the failure of his 1924 Munich *putsch*. It outlined his general ideas and philosophy, but in such general terms that its usefulness as evidence of his specific foreign policies is open to debate.

Munich agreement
: An agreement signed on 29 September 1938 by the leaders of Germany, Britain, France and Italy to resolve the dispute over the Sudetenland. The agreement handed the area over to Germany, transferred other areas of Czechoslovakia to Poland and Hungary, and guaranteed the rest of Czechoslovakia against attack. Neither Czechoslovakia nor the Soviet Union was invited to the conference. The meeting was the third between Hitler and Neville Chamberlain, who had earlier met at Berchtesgaden and Bad Godesburg to try to resolve the crisis.

Nazi–Soviet Pact
: An agreement between Nazi Germany and the Soviet Union negotiated by Ribbentrop and signed in Moscow on 23 August 1939. Each state agreed to remain neutral in any war the other might fight; secret clauses also divided Poland between them and allocated the Baltic States to the Soviet Union. Stalin remained loyal to the pact until the launch of Operation Barbarossa, the German invasion of the Soviet Union, on 22 June 1941.

Neutrality Acts
: A series of laws passed by the US Congress between 1935 and 1939, laying down a policy of neutrality in international affairs. The Acts prevented President Roosevelt from offering military assistance to Britain or France, but German attacks on American shipping led Congress to pass laws such as the Lend-Lease Act, which authorised non-military aid.

Night of the Long Knives

The 1934 coup in which Hitler eliminated Ernst Roehm and other leading figures within the SA, as well as many others of his political opponents. The killings were carried out by the SS, which thereby strengthened its grip on power.

Nuremberg Trial

A trial of leading Nazis held by a specially constituted International Military Tribunal, which consisted of judges from Britain, the United States, the USSR and France. The defendants were indicted on charges of war crimes, crimes against humanity, waging aggressive war and planning to wage aggressive war. The conduct of Nazi foreign policy was central to much of the trial.

Pact of Steel

A military alliance signed on 22 May 1939 between Germany and Italy. It reinforced the Rome-Berlin Axis.

Paris Peace Settlement

The correct term for the series of treaties signed in 1919 between the Allies and the defeated powers at the end of the First World War. The negotiations took place in Paris, and the treaties — formally signed in (and named after) a number of *châteaux* in the Paris region — included the Treaty of Versailles with Germany and the treaties of St Germain with Austria, Trianon with Hungary, Neuilly with Bulgaria and Sèvres with Turkey.

Plenipotentiary

A diplomatic representative with full powers to negotiate on behalf of his country. Other representatives are sometimes given only limited powers and have to refer matters of substance back to their home governments.

Polish Corridor

An area of West Prussia that was given to Poland under the terms of the Paris Peace Settlement. Its population was made up of some 500,000 Poles and some 300,000 Germans.

Popular Front

A term much used in the 1930s to denote a broad political coalition of left-wing groups, ranging from liberals to socialists, communists and even anarchists. Popular Fronts were the product of left-wing alarm at the rise of militant right-wing movements in the 1930s. Popular Front governments were elected in France in 1936 under Léon Blum and in Spain the same year, precipitating the Spanish Civil War.

Prussia

A German state that rose to prominence in the eighteenth century and rivalled Austria for the leadership of Germany in the nineteenth. The Prussian chancellor Otto von Bismarck unified the German states into a single Reich after the Franco–Prussian War of 1870–71. Although Prussia was often thought of as the quintessential German state, its policy of expansion into Poland in the eighteenth century had given it a substantial Polish population (see Polish Corridor).

Rapallo, Treaty of

A treaty signed in 1922 between Germany and the Soviet Union, which established trading relations between the two countries and secretly allowed German armaments firms and military units to operate deep in Russia, away from Allied inspection.

Reich

Often translated as 'empire', the word combines the English concepts of 'kingdom' and 'state'. The first Reich was the medieval German Holy Roman Empire. The second was the unified German empire declared in 1871 by Bismarck. The Weimar Republic retained the word Reich, and so, by declaring their regime the Third Reich, the Nazis undermined the Republic's status.

Reichswehr

The army of the Weimar Republic, commanded from 1920–26 by General Hans von Seeckt

Reparations

War damage payments, both in cost and materials, required of Germany under the terms of the Paris Peace Settlement. Reparations were principally paid to France, which insisted on strict adherence to the payment schedule. The schedule itself was revised in the 1924 Dawes and 1929 Young Plans.

Rhineland

The area between the Franco-German border and the river Rhine. Under the terms of the Treaty of Versailles it was to be occupied by Allied troops and German troops were forbidden to enter it. Stresemann negotiated the withdrawal first of British and then of French troops, after which the area was completely demilitarised until Hitler reoccupied it in 1936.

Rhineland Pact

An agreement negotiated by Stresemann with France and Belgium as part of the Locarno Treaties under which the three countries accepted their frontiers along the Rhine and agreed that the Rhineland should remain demilitarised. The treaty was signed by Britain and Italy as guarantors.

Rome–Berlin Axis

A pact of mutual cooperation signed between Germany and Italy in 1936. The name came from Mussolini's vision of an axis running between the two capitals around which the continent would revolve. It was not a formal military alliance; that was created by the 1939 Pact of Steel.

SA

Sturm Abteilung (storm troopers). Nazi paramilitary force led by Ernst Roehm, known from their uniform as 'brownshirts'. The SA's importance was greatly reduced after the 1934 Night of the Long Knives, in which many of its leaders, including Roehm, were murdered.

Saarland

An area of about 1,000 square miles around the river Saar and the town of Saarbrücken. Under the terms of the Treaty of Versailles the region's mines were controlled by France; the region itself was administered by the League of Nations. In 1935 a plebiscite was organised in the region; this resulted in a huge majority for reunion with Germany, which was immediately carried out.

Schlieffen Plan

Pre-1914 German war plan for attacking France via Belgium. The plan was put into operation in 1914 in a heavily modified form, bringing Britain into the war to defend Belgium, but petering out in the face of a French counter-offensive on the River Marne.

Spanish Civil War

Conflict of 1936–39, launched after the election in 1936 of a Popular Front government in Spain by an invasion from Spanish North Africa led by General Francisco Franco. As a conflict between opposing right- and left-wing philosophies, the war attracted volunteers from around the world. Britain and France maintained a policy of strict neutrality, but the Soviet Union sent financial and technical aid to the Republican government, Italy sent troops to help Franco and Germany sent the Condor Legion. Madrid finally fell to Franco's Nationalist forces in March 1939.

Spartacist League

A German socialist movement set up in 1915 by Rosa Luxemburg and Karl Liebknecht. The Spartacists opposed the First World War and in December 1918 founded the German Communist Party. Their attempt to set up a Soviet-style government in Berlin was put down by the *Freikorps*.

SPD

Sozialdemokratische Partei Deutschlands (Social Democratic Party of Germany), the German Socialist Party.

SS

Schutzstaffel (protective force). Nazi security force led by Heinrich Himmler. After the Night of the Long Knives it grew in importance, operating as an elite fighting force and running the network of concentration camps.

Stahlhelm

Literally 'steel helmet'. The largest and longest-lasting of the various paramilitary groups that made up the Freikorps. Although the Stahlhelm was strongly right-wing, its members did not all support the Nazis. In 1934 the Stahlhelm was incorporated into the SA.

Stresa Front

An agreement reached in 1935 by Italy, Britain and France to maintain a united front against German expansion and rearmament. It followed the failed German attempt to take over Austria in 1934 but was undermined by British and French opposition to the Italian invasion of Abyssinia later in 1935.

Sudetenland

A German-speaking area of the former Austro-Hungarian Empire south of its border with Germany. Under the terms of the Paris Peace Settlement, it was given to Czechoslovakia. In 1938 the German government encouraged the Sudeten Germans, under Konrad Henlein, to demand autonomy; when this was granted by the Karlsbad Programme, Hitler demanded that the region be handed over to Germany. This was finally provided for in the Munich agreement.

Teutonic knights

A medieval German crusading order, the Teutonic knights campaigned against the Poles and the pagans of Lithuania and led an invasion of Russia; as such they were regarded as heroes by the Nazis. The knights' defeat at the River Neva by the Russian leader Alexander Nevsky was similarly celebrated by the Russians in the aftermath of Operation Barbarossa.

Versailles, Treaty of

Treaty between the Allied powers and Germany, signed in 1919 as part of the Paris Peace Settlement. It imposed stringent limitations on Germany's territory and armed capacity; it also blamed Germany for having caused the war and therefore imposed heavy reparations, to recompense Allied nations, principally

France, for war damage. The injustice of the treaty, which the Germans had not been allowed to negotiate, was the cause of much bitterness and prompted many Germans to support the Nazis.

Wall Street Crash

US stock market collapse of October 1929 that precipitated the worldwide economic depression of the 1930s.

War-guilt clause

Article 231 of the 1919 Treaty of Versailles, stipulating that Germany bore full responsibility for starting the Great War. The clause was the justification for the treaty's harsh terms, and caused great bitterness in Germany.

Wehrmacht

The army of the Third Reich, so called to distinguish it from the *Reichswehr*.

Weimar Republic

The Republican government set up in Germany after the fall of the monarchy in November 1918. Officially called the Deutsches Reich, the republic was forever associated with the provincial town of Weimar where it was proclaimed, street fighting in Berlin having made the capital unsafe.

Winter War

The war sparked by the Soviet invasion of Finland in November 1939. The Finns fought the Red Army to a standstill, convincing Hitler that the conquest of the Soviet Union was feasible.

Young Plan

Agreement about German reparations negotiated in 1929 by US financier Owen D. Young with Stresemann. The plan reduced the total reparations bill by 25% and established a manageable schedule of payments with an end date of 1988.

Zollverein

'Customs union.' A free-trade area established among the German states in the 1830s. It was generally regarded as the precursor of political union in 1871 and therefore made Allied governments suspicious of plans for similar economic union between Germany and Austria in the 1920s and 1930s.